Portage: Pre-schoolers, Parents and Professionals
Ten Years of Achievement in the UK

Edited by
Robert J. Cameron

NFER-NELSON

Published by The NFER-NELSON Publishing Company Ltd.,
Darville House, 2 Oxford Road East,
Windsor, Berkshire SL4 1DF, England

and in the United States of America by

NFER-NELSON, 242 Cherry Street, Philadelphia, PA 19106 – 1906.
Tel: (215) 238 0939. Telex: 244489.

First Published 1986
© 1986 Robert J. Cameron

Library of Congress Cataloging in Publication data

Portage: pre-schoolers, parents, and professionals.
  Bibliography: p.
  1. Portage for handicapped children – Great Britain.
  2. Portage for handicapped children. I. Cameron, R.J. (Robert J.)
    LC4019.15.P67   1986   371.9   86–16322
    ISBN 0–7005–1073–7

Photoset in Times by David John Services Ltd, Maidenhead, Berks.

Printed by Billing & Sons Limited, Worcester

ISBN 0 7005 1073 7
Code 8251 02 1

309983

For Mollie White
a tireless champion of Portage

Contents

Foreword

David Shearer and Marsha Shearer

Marsha Shearer was Staff Training Coordinator and David Shearer was Project Director of the original Portage research team in Wisconsin.

It is indeed an honor to be given the opportunity to write the Foreword for this most impressive publication.

Seventeen years ago, we began the process of shaping a service system for young handicapped children and their families. In 1969, when the project was first funded by the United States Bureau of the Education for the Handicapped (later to become the Office of Special Education), we were committed to demonstrating one simple idea. It was that parents – with instruction, guidance and support – could teach their own children to grow and develop to their maximum potential. It never occurred to us that this idea would evolve into an internationally recognized early intervention model. This publication is testimony to the universal applicability of the model, but, more important, it is a tribute to *your* skill and commitment in adapting the Portage model to the needs and resources within your communities.

The Portage project obtained its name most fortuitously. It just happened to be the name of the small town in Wisconsin where the project was first developed. Portage Wisconsin, like most other 'Portages' in the world, received its name because it was a place which was a crossover, or portage, from a body of water to land. The name of the town was also a reflection of the project's basic mission. It was designed to serve as a bridge, a way of transferring skills and knowledge from professionals to parents; a way of bridging the gap between deficits exhibited by young children to skills needed for success in a school setting; a crossover from home to school. The name is just as appropriate in the British Isles because your intent now is the same as ours 17 years ago.

Although we are honored to write this Foreword, there are a number of professionals, paraprofessionals and parents who should share in the recognition for the project's creation. The original developers, pioneers if you will, were a group of professionals who had neither background in early childhood education nor in parent training. They comprised a group of creative special educators, regular educators and psychologists who shared the ambitious task of developing a model that would (a) provide comprehensive services to young handicapped children and their families in the child's natural environment – the home, (b) be complex in design yet simple in its implementation, (c) be easily replicated by programs that were without a wide array of human and fiscal resources, and (d) demonstrate that parents from a variety of backgrounds and with a variety of child rearing beliefs could indeed effectively teach their own children. We take this opportunity to recognize our colleagues who helped develop the Portage model. Each person contributed a little piece of themselves that when added together resulted in media, training materials, data management systems, research studies, reports, articles, additional funding and replication sites. These replication sites generated new adaptations and new materials. Each of you is part of this network of committed, skilled and caring people. We thank you. Ultimately, of course, it is parents and families that make the system work. It was their willingness to try something new and their basic sense of confidence and self-worth that allowed them to take the leap of faith.

Never in our wildest dreams or fantasies did any of us foresee the growth, the popularity and the massive adoptions and adaptations that would take place. We remember the excitement about our first replication site – in a town 50 miles away from Portage. Today, the project is still in operation in Portage, Wisconsin, and the Portage model is still expanding, continuing to be molded and shaped to meet the unique needs and differences in communities throughout the United States and the world. The Portage project has been replicated in hundreds of communities in the United States. It has provided assistance to replication efforts in countries such as Peru, Colombia, Equador, Jamaica, Japan, Canada, Mexico, India, Guam, the Philippines, Puerto Rico, the Dominican Republic, and most recently in the Gaza Strip and the West Bank. The newest potential site is China. However, the most exhaustive and complete adoption and adaptation effort is found here in the United Kingdom.

In 1976, we responded to a request by Dr Albert Kushlick of Wessex and Dr Roger Blunden of Wales for two consultants to conduct a series of workshops that described the components and practices of the Portage Model. We elected to send Betsy May and George Jesien as our first representatives to the United Kingdom. They were followed by Susie Frohman and Dick Boyd in 1977 and Neal Schortinghuis and Deborah Cochran in 1979. Each team returned with news of current developments of the Portage system in the United Kingdom. From the start, it was clear that a group of competent and dedicated professionals would take this planted seed and nurture its growth in its new and unique environment.

This publication is evidence that the Portage project has become the United Kingdom's Portage scheme. We salute you for all of the most impressive and exhaustive expansions and improvements that have been made to the system through the years. It is your critical involvement that will continue to shape the project's future.

CHAPTER 1
Portage: Pre-schoolers, Parents and Professionals

Robert J. Cameron

Tutor for Advanced Professional Training in Educational Psychology at Southampton University and a founder member of the Winchester Portage Home Teaching Service.

In April 1976 a somewhat unusual project for families who had a pre-school child with special needs was set up in Winchester, Hants. The extraordinary nature of this service was reflected in a number of features, most of which had at that time rarely figured in previous services for this client group. In the first place, the venture had occurred as a result of more than ten years' applied research which had been carried out by the Wessex Health Care Evaluation Research Team. The new service was home based, used parents as teachers and involved a variety of different personnel from health, social services and education and the voluntary sector working together. Finally, the service was not only self-evaluative but also had a built-in accountability component.

In many ways, this new service represented a break with traditional attempts to help families who had pre-school children with special educational needs, since it was not merely grafted on to traditional models of service used for older children and even more surprisingly, in what was in the mid-1970s viewed as a somewhat radical approach, it did not take the children out of their homes to help them: instead the service was delivered to parents in their homes.

The Portage home teaching scheme originated at the University of Wisconsin in 1969 and was set up as a result of the Handicapped Children's Early Education Assistance Act, the purpose of which was 'to test and establish innovative early education programmes for handicapped children, which might lead to comprehensive models that could be replicated by others' (see Jesien (1984) for a description of this early development). Early success ensured that it became one of a tiny number of several hundred research projects which was recommended by the Federal Bureau for the Mentally Handicapped as being 'an exemplary service for handicapped pre-schoolers'. During the 1970s the Portage home teaching model was replicated extensively and by 1984 there were over 140 sites in the United States and Canada (Jesien, *op. cit.*). Successful Portage schemes had also been set up in a number of South American, Asian and European countries (Jesien, *op. cit.*).

The first UK project, the Wessex Portage Research Project, was set up by the Wessex Health Care Evaluation Research Team in 1976 in Winchester. This pilot scheme had 13 families, three home teachers, a supervisor and a small management team and once again the early results were encouraging (see Smith *et al.* (1977) for detailed results of the first six months of this scheme). Similarly encouraging results were also obtained on a sister research project in South Glamorgan (Revill and Blunden, 1979a). From these somewhat modest beginnings, the Portage scheme has spread to more than 150 sites throughout the British Isles (Bendall *et al.*, 1984).

The Portage model

The Portage approach is designed to help parents of children with special educational needs to teach their own children in their own homes. This objective is achieved by home teachers from a variety of supporting professional groups including teachers, health visitors, community nurses, family service workers, therapists and volunteers, who visit each family weekly and teach parents how to use carefully planned direct instructional techniques with their children. The resulting activity programme is not only designed to meet the educational needs of each individual child in a particular home setting but also provides an ongoing record of the child's progress.

The central feature of Portage is the home teaching process. On their weekly visits, home teachers identify and agree new skills which parents would like their developmentally delayed child to acquire and also agree interventions for teaching these skills. These teaching strategies are not only clearly written down but also demonstrated by the home teacher then tried out by the parent while the home teacher is still present to give advice if necessary. Such procedures ensure that the parent is familiar with the teaching task before the home teacher leaves the home.

No child is too handicapped to be accepted on to a scheme and home teaching continues on a weekly basis until the child goes to school.

Families with problems

The birth of a child is an event which changes every family. Most families make some minor adjustments and are able to continue with a fairly normal lifestyle. However, there are a minority of families who have an exceptional child and for them the change in lifestyle is sometimes dramatic and is often a prolonged process. Some of the successes and problems of parents who have a handicapped child are clearly and often movingly detailed by the parents themselves, e.g. Russell (1983), Philps (1984), Lloyd (1986).

Very often, the major problems faced by parents are the seemingly minor aspects of family life that are almost taken for granted, e.g. playing with other children, getting dressed and undressed, acquiring appropriate eating skills, communicating with other children and adults, or, as a child nears school age, learning pre-school skills like copying, colouring, matching and so on. In addition, many pre-school children who have moderate or severe learning difficulties may exhibit behaviours which can be a considerable disruption to family life. Problem behaviours include biting a younger brother or sister, screaming when not picked up, having temper outbursts in crowded supermarkets, waking many times each night, throwing objects and so on.

The twin problems of *learning* and *behaviour* difficulties exhibited by handicapped children are well documented and this deficit–excess problem classification is described in detail in Gardner (1977) and has been used extensively by a number of applied researchers (see especially Kushlick *et al.*, 1978).

The parents

Child rearing has been described as 'a dialogue between parents and children' (Wolfendale, 1985a) yet until quite recently this dialogue has been considered unimportant, has gone largely unrecorded and has generally been ignored by researchers.

There are many reasons why the last decade may yet become known as the period when parents were 'rediscovered'. Such reasons include research evidence as to the effectiveness of parents as teachers of the handicapped children (Bronfenbrenner, 1974), the highlighting of the parental contribution by early education by government reports (e.g. Court, 1976; Warnock, 1978) and recent legislation, especially the 1981 Education Act, which has enhanced parental involvement in assessment and treatment of children with special needs.

The trend towards increased parental involvement is most clearly illustrated in recent publications aimed at supporting professionals in health, social services and education. While Lansdowne (1980) concentrated on the identification of the 'everyday needs of sick and handicapped children and their families', Mittler and McConachie (1983) went further and discussed some 'approaches to partnership between parents, professionals and mentally handicapped people'. Even more recently, Griffiths and Russell (1985) offered concrete guidelines for parents and professionals on how to 'work together with handicapped children'.

The viewpoint that parents are the 'major educators of their children in the early years' (Warnock, *op. cit.*) is now widely recognized as well as supported by the research literature.

Support professionals

Despite the evidence for the home as an effective learning environment, both *indirect contact* professionals, e.g. psychologists, doctors, therapists, social workers and *direct contact* professionals, e.g. teaching, nursing and child care staff, often appear to be reluctant to involve parents as equal partners in the education of their handicapped children. Even today, many professionals appear to hold the view that educating handicapped children is best left to the 'experts' and often this standpoint is justified by somewhat spurious arguments like 'parents need to be prevented from getting over-involved' or even 'parents need frequent breaks from their handicapped child'.

Indeed, in the case of some services set up to help families with a pre-school handicapped child, it has even been argued that many services have operated as though the home did not exist (except of course as a source of problems!) (Cameron, 1984a).

Pilling (1973), in her notable review of more than two decades of research, was able to show that the lack of practical advice or emotional support from services outside the family was an almost universal experience of parents who had a handicapped pre-schooler. Sadly too, in a follow-up report in 1981 she had to record that although professionals were more 'aware' of these problems, many 'service deficits' still remained.

In fact, there is a considerable amount of evidence in the literature to suggest that many parents of handicapped children are *less than satisfied* with the services which they receive from supporting professionals.

In particular, parents complained that they were given very little practical advice on helping the handicapped child to become a member of the family (Spain and Wigley, 1975), or advice on the management of disruptive behaviour (Pilling, *op. cit.*). Parents further reported that the problems which they raised as important were frequently ignored or dismissed by support professionals (Cooper and Henderson, 1973; Gath, 1978, etc.).

Cunningham (1977) reported that a considerable number of parents who had young children with Down's syndrome described the services which they had received from both visiting and non-visiting professionals as 'not very helpful'. From an analysis of their comments, it appeared that parents 'really wanted to know what they could do immediately to help their child' and often felt isolated from their child because they could not help the handicapped member of their family 'as they do their other children'.

Not surprisingly therefore, many parents of pre-school children with special needs have highlighted the relatively poor relationships which can exist between themselves and supporting professionals in health, social services and education who are all too often perceived by parents as insensitive, remote and occasionally downright tactless (Lloyd-Bostock, 1976; Reid, 1979; Ferguson and Watt, 1980, etc.).

Problem summary

The problems facing parents, professionals and pre-school children with special needs can therefore be summarized as follows:

(a) Children with special needs find difficulty in learning new skills and/or exhibit disruptive behaviour which may either prevent learning or obscure more appropriate behaviour.

(b) Parents find difficulty in teaching their handicapped pre-schoolers and in managing their disruptive behaviour.

(c) Supporting professionals are not always able to help parents to help their children.

Against the backcloth of these well-established problem areas the Portage service was set up.

Portage home teaching

At first sight the Portage approach appears to be an unusually simple one. A home teacher visits each family weekly and discusses with parents important skills they would like their children to learn. Working closely together, this 'home team' agrees a method of teaching these skills which is carefully matched to the personality and needs of the child in the family setting. All agreed teaching activities are written down on an *activity chart* which remains with the parent for one week.

Before leaving the home, the Portage home teacher demonstrates each activity to the parent and then observes the parent trying out teaching activities with the child and offers advice if necessary. As agreed, the parent practises and records the outcome of teaching trials during the remainder of the week, until the home teacher returns one week later to check out with the parent that the child has been able to carry out the new skills.

To enable the home teacher to deliver a high quality service, three Portage job aids have been designed. These are:

1 *The Portage Checklist.* This is used to identify the child's existing repertoire of skills and to select future teaching objectives in the following areas – self-help, motor, language, social and cognitive developments. In addition, there is a section of 'infant stimulation' activities which can be used either with very young children or older children who have acquired very few skills.

This checklist (Bluma *et al.*, 1976) is used as both an initial and ongoing assessment procedure and is the basis for selecting future teaching objectives.

2 *The Portage Teaching Cards.* This card file provides specific teaching instructions for each of the 600-odd items on the Portage checklist. These cards have two main functions – providing useful teaching hints particularly for new or inexperienced home teachers and providing suggestions on different ways of teaching the same skill and thus enabling the child to generalize and adapt the skills being taught.

3 *The Portage Activity Chart.* This is a carefully designed procedure which allows parents to teach their child and also to record the results of their teaching efforts. Each activity chart is written to a carefully worked out formula, which not only specifies what has to be taught but how it is to be taught, with what level of success and how progress is to be recorded (see Cameron (1979) for details).

Although it appears very simple, the Portage activity chart is a highly sophisticated teaching method, a point which is discussed in detail by Faūpel and Cameron (1984).

Positive monitoring

The positive monitoring component has been built into the Portage model to allow a supervisor to receive detailed reports from home teachers on the teaching carried out by parents. At a weekly or fortnightly staff meeting, the results of successful teaching are shared. In addition, any problems relating to the acquisition of agreed teaching targets (educational problems) or difficulties which have arisen in the family (family problems), or problems which involve other supporting professionals who supply services to the family (agency problems) may be clarified and interventions agreed and monitored.

A final stage of the monitoring is the three-monthly management team meeting where representatives from health, social services, education, the voluntary sector and the Portage parents meet to hear a report prepared by the supervisor. This lists the services successfully provided by home teachers to parents and also allows members of the management team to clarify and suggest interventions to problems which have occurred, especially those requiring solutions which can only be implemented at higher levels of management. Forward planning and policy making are also carried out by the management team.

Portage: a summary

The Portage home teaching model has three key features:

1   Using *direct contact people* (especially parents) to teach children who have special needs.
2   Using *direct instructional methods.* Carnine (1979) describes Direct Instructional (DI) programmes as being characterized by 'increasing teaching time, carefully designed curricula, direct teaching procedures, quality control and active parental involvement'. A major advantage of the DI model is that it is a highly effective teaching method which appears to out-perform other methods of teaching (see Becker *et al.* (1981) and Carnine, *op. cit.,* for details).
3   Using *positive monitoring and recording* procedures. One of the highly valued features of the Portage model is the way in which it can help people who are directly involved, e.g. parents and home teachers, as well as supporting professionals (doctors, therapists, psychologists, etc.) who are indirectly involved, to respond to carefully collected data about the progress of children on the receiving end of this service.

Portage can therefore be seen as a problem-centred service delivery system which enables parents to carry out sophisticated direct instructional procedures with their children. This service is supported by a self-evaluation component which allows service delivery to be maintained and continuously improved.

Some results

The results of the early work in Wisconsin (Shearer and Shearer, 1972) together with the number of important evaluation studies in the UK (Smith *et al., op. cit.*; Revill and Blunden, 1979a; Barna *et al.*, 1980; etc.) have demonstrated that Portage can help parents to teach their handicapped children. The success with which home teachers and parents carry out these activities can be judged by the fact that most schemes report that over 90 per cent of agreed activities are successfully attained each week (Cameron, 1984a).

Feedback from the consumers has been positive. Parents have said that home teachers help them to teach their child important useful life skills and where necessary devise management strategies for disruptive behaviour. Parents also say that as well as practical help, they have received help with family and agency problems. Not surprisingly therefore parents have unhesitatingly recommended the Portage service to other families with a handicapped pre-schooler. It is worth noting that, even today, parents are often less enthusiastic about other services which they and their children receive!

The positive monitoring component has not only ensured quality control but has also encouraged service improvement. As well as making some improvements to the original Portage model which was imported from the United States, new teaching packages have been developed on the following topics: long-term curriculum planning, managing disruptive behaviour, working with supporting professionals, examining the home teaching process and promoting high quality learning. These topics are now incorporated into the three-day basic training workshop provided for Portage home teachers.

Since the activities required of management team members, the supervisors, home teachers, parents and children are carefully detailed, Portage home teaching schemes (unlike most research projects for pre-schoolers) have been remarkably easy to replicate. In short, the Portage approach has worked just as well in Warrington, Westmorland and Walthamstow as it has done in Winchester! (See details of the National Portage Survey carried out by Bendall *et al.*, 1984.)

Another interesting demonstration of the robustness of the Portage model has been the way it has been adapted to meet widely different local demands. This has meant that while most services have used professionals from health, social services and education as home teachers, variations of this original model appear to enjoy equal success. Some projects have used parent volunteers as home teachers (Ellender, 1982), others have had only one Portage worker in a centre-based setting (Cook, 1982), while a number of schemes have been school based (see especially Hallmark and Dessent, 1982) or adapted for a pre-school playgroup (Clark and Cameron, 1983).

As well as operating in different settings using a wide variety of personnel, the Portage model has been tried out with a variety of different client groups including children exhibiting severe behaviour problems (Prosser, 1982), physically handicapped pupils (Dyer and Huggett, 1984) and handicapped adults (Jenkins, 1982, and Tyerman and Sewpaul, 1983). A recent study examined the feasibility of introducing Portage to Asian families who had a pre-school mentally handicapped child (Powell and Perkins, 1984). Their conclusion was that linking a scheme such as Portage to mother tongue speaking home visitors might be the most suitable way of providing the support which these parents needed to teach their children.

Additional advantages

It is clear that the Portage home teaching model represents a low cost, highly effective way of helping parents to deal with the everyday problems of bringing up a handicapped child. However, the Portage approach possesses a number of other noteworthy features:

The *Pyramid model* of working within the Portage framework can be seen as an economic use of scarce professional time since it allows thinly spread management team members and supervisors to remove themselves from direct intervention, yet continue to monitor in detail the services provided by home teachers and the activities carried out by the parents.

The majority of problems encountered by families are successfully dealt with *at home* (or if necessary at a staff meeting). Only rarely does the management team have to tackle outstanding problems: yet another saving on scarce professional time.

Accountability is built into a Portage service since the positive monitoring system allows everyone to see clearly whether management team members, supervisors, home teachers and parents have carried out the tasks which they have agreed to do. This is a particularly interesting aspect since it immediately overcomes the so called 'professional–parent dichotomy'. Portage utilizes the detailed knowledge of parents and the specialist knowledge of supporting professionals. This means that parents and supporting professionals not only have clearly defined roles within the service but can also recognize that each is a vital component in the handicapped child's upbringing.

The Portage model recognizes that children gain most from education when *parents* are closely involved in the teaching. Until now, many administrators and policy makers seeking to help severely handicapped children and their families have often looked for service improvements outside the home, e.g. smaller classes, purpose-built centres, sophisticated aids, complex teaching methods, etc. Portage is a good example of a service which readily concedes that among the many experts working with the pre-school handicapped child, the most useful and effective are the ones which nature provided – the parents themselves!

An overview

As a result of a paper entitled 'A National Portage Home Teaching Association: is there a need for one?' presented at the Second National Portage Conference in Cambridge, a National Portage Association was set up (Kushlick, 1984). The Association, which represents Portage services from all over the British Isles has applied itself to drawing up guidelines for setting up and maintaining Portage schemes. It is hoped that these guidelines will help existing projects to maintain their standard of service delivery and provide standards for newly emerging schemes.

The Portage model is a highly sophisticated service for parents and other people who spend long periods of time in contact with children who have special educational needs. The core components of a Portage approach – parental involvement, structured teaching and positive monitoring – allow home teachers to help parents to teach their handicapped offspring important new life skills and where necessary manage disruptive behaviour (and back up this help with ongoing evaluation which ensures both continuity and quality control). The result: nearly ten years later Portage continues to grow, improve and develop.

CHAPTER 2
Experiencing Portage: An Account by a Parent and a Home Teacher

Linda Jordan and Sheila Wolfendale

Linda Jordan is a schoolteacher and a parent on the Newham Portage Service. Sheila Wolfendale is Tutor to the MSc (Educational Psychology) Course at North East London Polytechnic and a coordinator of the Newham Portage Service.

Part 1: A parent's story

Ellen was born in September 1982 in the London Hospital, Whitechapel, and was immediately diagnosed as having Down's syndrome. With that diagnosis came what I now see as the continuing contradiction of mental handicap.

On the one hand, mental handicap is seen by some people as a tragedy or disaster and the mother who gives birth to a mentally handicapped baby is therefore to be pitied, sympathized with, mollycoddled, ignored, worried about and feared.

On the other hand, there is the view that giving birth to a mentally handicapped child means that your life will be enriched and full of love. In a sense, you are even seen as privileged, since everyone wants to help handicapped children and 'they are only sent to those who can cope', etc.

Not surprisingly, I felt very confused by the different messages I received in those early days. I suspected then and now know that both sets of attitudes are absurd. I had had an enjoyable pregnancy, a satisfying labour and delivery and my beautiful new baby was very much wanted and welcomed by my husband and myself. At that time I was happy, yet society seemed to be telling me that Ellen's handicap should overshadow my real feelings.

The nursing officer in the hospital gave me some literature from the Down's Children's Association, together with the name and telephone number of a parent contact in my home area. When I came home from hospital, my husband rang the parent contact and she said that she would visit.

Anna's visit was a breath of fresh air. Here was another person who had a Down's daughter: she was obviously happy and made it clear through her words and actions that her life was functioning in a very ordinary way. Laura, just like her other children, had brought joy but also occasional sorrow.

Anna explained that Down's children do learn, but that a different approach is needed towards their learning. She brought a social worker with her and between them they told us about the local support services. Portage was discussed and Anna explained the benefits and how home teaching works. Portage seemed like good sense, so we said we would like to start as soon as possible.

On the 1st December, when Ellen was ten weeks old, Annette visited us. She became Ellen's Portage home visitor for a year.

The first Portage year

On her introductory visit Annette explained the ideas behind Portage. A Portage checklist was produced and it was suggested that I should begin to tick off the items in the 'Infant Stimulation' section Ellen was already doing, and use these as a starting point for teaching. We looked through the checklist and decided that for the first week we would work on 'child turns head to sound'. Annette showed me the activity chart and together we worked out exactly what we would do. We decided on six trials a day.

For the rest of the week my husband or I did the trials each day and although it may not sound very significant to the reader of this chapter, we gained tremendous satisfaction from carrying out these small tasks with Ellen. When she turned her head for the first time it was wonderful and by the end of the week Ellen turned her head every time we rang the little bell. This activity chart is reproduced in Figure 1.

Somehow that first Portage week gave me so much hope. I felt confident that as long as we all thought carefully about what we were doing and made sure that our teaching targets were realistic, it

Figure 1: Ellen's first Activity Chart

Checklist number *12*
Child's name *Ellen*
Home Teacher's name *Annette*
Week of *7.12.82*

BEHAVIOUR
*Ellen will turn her eyes
and head in direction
of sound*

CRITERIA: *6/6 trials*

NUMBER OF
*Times Ellen turns eyes
and head in direction
of sound*

	TU	WE	TH	FR	SA	SU	MO
6	(✓)L	(✓)L	✓L	✓L	✓L	✓L	✓L
5	✓R	✓	(✓)R	(✓)R	✓R	(✓)R	✓R
4	(✓)L	(✓)L	✓L	✓L	✓L	✓L	✓L
3	✓R	✓R	✓R	(✓)R	✓R	(✓)R	✓R
2	✓L	(✓)L	✓L	✓L	✓L	✓L	✓L
1	✓R	✓R	✓R	(✓)R	✓R	✓R	✓R

DIRECTIONS: *Lie Ellen on the floor on her back. Use a rattle, bell, tissue paper, anything that makes a noise. Hold the noise maker to either side of her and shake or rattle it. Make sure it is loud enough for her to hear. Say 'Ellen, look'. When she turns towards the sound praise her saying 'Good girl' and smiling. Randomly make the sounds in different places and gradually increase the distance between the sound source and Ellen.*
REINFORCEMENT: *Say 'Good girl' and smile.*
CORRECTION PROCEDURE: *If Ellen needs help to find the sound, gently move her head towards the sound.*
RECORD: *When Ellen turns towards the sound on her own, mark that trial with ✓ on the chart. If you need to give help then mark trial on the chart (✓)*
Mark R or L next to the task dependent on whether Ellen turned her eyes and head to right or left.

would be possible to teach Ellen many of the skills which all children learn.

Over the weeks and months Annette became an important part of our family life. It was therefore very sad when she had to leave us. Annette had been a post-graduate on the Educational Psychology course at North East London Polytechnic and in September 1983 she left to start her new job as an educational psychologist.

The first year of home teaching had been a very positive experience. By now Ellen was standing up holding on to our furniture and beginning to 'cruise'. She also had a keen interest in sitting and playing with her bricks and other toys.

Other support people

Throughout the year, Annette had sought the advice of both physiotherapist and speech therapist. Ellen's physiotherapist Sandra had first visited our home when Ellen was just a few weeks old. She offered advice about Ellen's motor development and demonstrated exercises to strengthen neck muscles. Sandra visited us at home for the first few months until I started to take Ellen to the physiotherapy group at the Child Development Centre. At that group, Ellen not only continued to be seen by Sandra, but also learned to play alongside and eventually with other children. Ellen and I also joined the weekly baby and toddler swimming session run by the physiotherapists.

When Ellen was about eight months old, Pauline, our speech therapist, invited me to take Ellen to a language group at a local special school. There I was told about the Makaton signing system and given advice on games to play and encourage early language development. The advice given by the physiotherapist and speech therapist was invaluable and we could also incorporate it into our Portage teaching programme.

The second and third years

Ellen's new Portage home visitor was Sheila Wolfendale, who started working with us in January 1984. There was therefore a three-month 'gap' in Ellen's Portage programme. These months were very frustrating for me, my husband and, I think, for Ellen too.

At that time, Ellen seemed to be on the threshold of acquiring so many important skills, but I could not see how to help her. She had been keen to be on her feet for so many months and by Christmas 1983 she seemed to be very near to walking. She was also making sounds and wanted to feed and drink by herself. So many people said that she would do all these things 'in her own good time' and that there was nothing I could do to help. I did not believe this, but I didn't really know what to do: I needed both advice and support which Portage had previously provided.

When Sheila first visited she must have felt inundated with the things that I wanted to work on. She probably thought that I had totally unrealistic expectations for Ellen: walking, talking, feeding herself, etc. If she did have such doubts, Sheila appeared undaunted, and together we worked out short-term targets aimed at helping Ellen to acquire many of my long-term goals.

As a result, during the next 18 months, Ellen learned to feed herself, drink from an open cup, walk, draw and paint and she started walking. Although I am now sure that she would have done all these things – eventually – I am certain that working within the Portage programme enabled Ellen to acquire these skills much sooner than she would otherwise have done. This has been important not only because it made her life (and mine) easier in a society which does not put itself out for handicapped people, but also it reduced her frustrations. Being able to communicate her thoughts and feelings has given Ellen self-confidence, self-worth and independence.

Occasionally, we did not set a new target for the week, but instead we used the time for revision or consolidation. During these weeks I would write a review of all the targets which had been set in the previous period and make sure that Ellen could still do these. As Annette had done during the first year, Sheila had contact with other people working with Ellen. In particular, she sought advice from Pauline, Ellen's speech therapist, because we were doing quite a lot of language work.

Benefits of Portage

The obvious and most important benefit for our family is that Ellen has acquired so many skills. She has grown up knowing that 'working' for a short time each day is a part of her life. She enjoys performing her target trials and sitting down at her table and doing things in general. (I consider the latter to be an important skill in itself!)

For me, receiving support and advice of a very practical nature in my own home was the most helpful aspect of Portage. My weekly visits from the home visitor have always been very important, but in the early days they were vital. I needed someone to help me to teach my child. I knew that she could learn because I could see the other Down's children learning, but I didn't know how to help her. I knew that I could read the many books on the subject of mental handicap yet I did not want the fact that I had a handicapped child to take over my life. I needed someone to tell me what sorts of things a non-handicapped child of Ellen's age would be doing and to give me some ideas about how to teach Ellen to do those things. That is exactly what Portage has done.

As time has gone on, my needs have changed. Gradually I have begun to feel more and more an expert about Ellen's development and educational needs. I feel that I have had a three-year training course in special education and indeed I have recently begun teaching in a school for mentally handicapped children. My Portage experience has made me feel at home with children who have special educational needs and I also feel that I have acquired a useful background knowledge in child development.

In June 1984 our second child, Michael, was born. Going through the milestones with a non-handicapped child has been fascinating and exciting and has made it clear why a structured learning programme is so important for Ellen. Michael seems to learn automatically, whereas Ellen needs help to discover new things.

Although many of the benefits of Portage could probably have been achieved by another teaching approach, the Portage 'method' is exceedingly cost-effective: the maximum results can be achieved with the minimum amount of effort. Since even the most complex skills can be broken down into very small stages, no target is unapproachable. By looking at the present skill level and what the child *can* do, realistic targets *towards* a long-term goal can be set. The structured record keeping of daily trials means that after a period of time it is possible for parents and home teachers to see progress and even when it seems that there has been little progress, the record sheets can show otherwise. By carrying out so many trials a day you know that you are helping your child even though this may only take ten minutes. This positive programme can help to avoid the guilt that parents of handicapped children often feel about not helping their children enough.

Parent training

In my local area there has been a recent initiative in parent training, and a programme of training for parents who will be included in the Newham Portage scheme in the future has been set up. This ingenious scheme seeks to use the expertise of parents who have been receiving Portage to train new parents.

I feel that my Portage training has been gradual throughout the three years. I have enjoyed gaining expertise and am sure that Ellen's home visitors have gained the practical experience to complement their Portage training course. In retrospect, I think that I would have welcomed a short introductory training course if it had been available. I think that I relied too much on the home visitor in the early days and some training might have avoided that need.

Ellen's statement

By the time Ellen was two, we had decided to ask her 'special educational needs' to be assessed under section 5 of the 1981 Education Act. We thought that it was necessary to go through this procedure because we believed that Ellen's needs should be defined and the educational provision she needed should be formally recorded. We did not want the available special education provisions to determine what sort of school Ellen would go to nor did we want her to be permanently 'on trial', as she would be if she went to the local nursery school without a statement.

When Ellen was two weeks old we had been told by a health authority paediatrician that she would go to a school for the 'severely educationally subnormal'. At two, Ellen was not in our opinion 'severely educationally subnormal'; however, she clearly had special educational needs. We thought that she should attend the local primary school and her special needs should be met there.

Our Portage experience meant that we were able with confidence to write our contribution to the statement procedures (see Appendix I).

Our contribution turned out to be more comprehensive and detailed than any of the professional advice written about our daughter. This bears out my belief that parents who work with their children become 'experts'.

An update on Ellen

Ellen started at our local nursery school in January 1986 and her statement says that she will continue to receive the support of an LEA home liaison teacher. Pauline Condron, Ellen's home liaison teacher, has been working with Ellen at home since March 1985. In the last few weeks of the autumn term she accompanied Ellen to the nursery for one preparatory afternoon a week.

The work which Pauline has been doing with Ellen does not conflict with Portage, but like the other supporting services we have received tends to complement home teaching.

Ellen's new Portage home visitor, Richard, has been visiting us since early December. We spent some time working on 'opposites': trying to teach Ellen the difference between 'wet' and 'dry' and 'boy' and 'girl'. Such objectives were chosen very much with school in mind.

In February 1985 Ellen began to read. A year earlier, Sheila Wolfendale had shown us an article about the work of Sue Buckley at Portsmouth Polytechnic who had been teaching young Down's children to read. As a result of this article (Buckley, 1985) we began the reading programme and by December Ellen was reading about 80 words from flashcards and had begun to read simple phrases. At first I thought that reading should be incorporated in the Portage programme, but in the event it was not necessary to have activity charts for reading targets as Ellen learned to read her words so easily. In fact word recognition was the easiest skill that we taught Ellen. I do think, however, that it was our background in Portage that gave us the confidence to start the reading project with Ellen and to work within a structured teaching situation.

Ellen's speech has improved dramatically since she started to read: it was, however, Portage which got Ellen's speech going in the first place. By using the Portage 'approach', it was clear from an early stage that Ellen's receptive language was well developed. Knowing this, we were able to encourage language development at the earliest opportunity and Ellen's first clear words were the result of carefully planned Portage activity charts.

In short, the Portage home teaching service gave me confidence that my child could learn and it gave me the confidence to teach her. Working with the Portage framework meant that we could see exactly how Ellen was developing and in which areas she needed most help. For me, Portage has made the slogan 'Parents as Partners' into a reality. I only hope that that reality can continue once Ellen goes to school!

Part 2: The home teacher's story

In September 1983 the embryonic Newham Portage venture metamorphosed into an 'official' scheme, fulfilling basic criteria in terms of management structure, supervision systems, various forms of record keeping, and with the first proper Portage training.

The Newham Portage started out and has remained as a unique blend of trainee and experienced practitioners. There is an explicit link between the Master's Degree (MSc) professional training course for educational psychologists and personnel from Newham's statutory services. Annually the trainee educational psychologists on this one-year course receive their three-day Portage training alongside members of the mental handicap team, speech therapists, teachers, nursery nurses, clinical psychology trainees and others. The trainees become home visitors on the scheme, which is at present jointly organized and coordinated by the MSc Educational Psychology Course Tutor (this author) and one of the (currently) two home liaison teachers within the Education Department.

I received my Portage training in the autumn of 1983, and acknowledged, when I 'inherited' Ellen, that I was about to work with parents who had at that point superior first-hand knowledge of goal and target setting, and task analysis. Thus I had an instant introduction to the principle, of what I had defined (Wolfendale, 1983) as 'equivalent expertise'. My general knowledge of child development and experience as an educational psychologist were complemented by Linda Jordan and Chris Goodey's *intimate* knowledge of Ellen and their developed skills of appraising and planning her next 'developmental tasks', within a context, not only of progress to date, but of her own pace of learning and responsiveness.

Working with Ellen

As a psychologist, who for longer than now seems tenable had operated within the traditional mantle of casework with a somewhat random timetable of home visits, the regularity of Portage home visiting had a spin-off of developing professional competence in planning, maintenance, and some cognitive rigour. The discipline is imposed from without by the Portage structure, and from the requirement to be consistent, task-focused, and analytic.

An early planning and organizational priority of mine was to ensure, within a crowded and mobile job brief, that regularity of weekly visiting would be maintained. This turned out to be possible, with gaps in visiting being accounted for in the main by holidays or illness. The number of visits over the 18-month period was over 60.

Record keeping

It may be an indication of the flexibility of the Portage model that, in any one locality, the record forms in use reflect adherence to Portage criteria as well as local requirements. Record keeping by Ellen's parents and myself was, as it was with the whole Newham Portage, just such a mix. It comprised:

Home visitor's initial data sheet: on this is recorded basic 'entry' details of a child and his/her situation, referral to agencies and other treatment being received. This form provides the first opportunity to record (subject to later modification) short- and longer-term goals.

Activity chart: we had compared various activity charts in use, and had preferred one which had been in use in the Barking and Dagenham Portage Service.

Checklist and the Wessex Revised Portage Language Checklist: Ellen's parents updated the checklist upon my arrival, and they were introduced to the more detailed Wessex Language Checklist. We evolved a practice whereby these were updated every three months. Ellen's general developmental, as well as Portage progress could thus be regularly appraised, using the items as checkpoints. The information was also used to help set short- and long-term goals (see below).

Longer-term goal sheet: this was introduced into Newham Portage during 1984–85, so was incorporated into our work with Ellen towards the end of my stint as home visitor.

Home visitor's record sheet: this comprises the weekly record, in terms of targets reached, renewed, revised or abandoned; relevant current information on Ellen or family circumstances, and summary comments.

Recapitulation: we found it helpful to have occasional (2) retrospective checks on successful targets, to check on maintenance, to ensure, in addition to incidentally 'knowing', that certain behaviours were still observably part of Ellen's repertoire. Linda and Chris recorded their checks and outcomes in written form.

Target and goal setting

Parental completion of the checklists was used in conjunction with the parents' own observations of Ellen in situ at home and in naturally occurring situations. Thus as parents they were continually assessing Ellen's pace of learning, her responsiveness, her interest, and her learning needs. So we did not rely exhaustively upon checklists to generate targets – they tended to arise 'naturally' from domestic routine and family activities. It is important to take account, for decision making, of the interplay between a child's developmental status, opportunities for learning within his/her environment and the overall family context. A behaviourally-oriented approach to learning can and ought to be consistent with ecological perspectives!

Over the 18-month period, the targets covered major areas of development and skill, as can be seen in the listing below.

Ellen's progress

TARGETS ACHIEVED BETWEEN JANUARY 1984 AND JULY 1985

Each target was achieved within one, two or three weeks. The activity charts and other record sheets show length of time taken, also whether or not a given target was revised before eventual mastery.

'Unsuccessful' targets were those which were abandoned when lack of mastery was due to factors such as

(i)   Ellen's lack of interest
(ii)   Ellen's lack of cooperation
(iii) the task proved to be too difficult
(iv)   Ellen was not yet 'ready' for this activity ⎫ despite setting a baseline

The targets achieved are presented below in the approximate sequence in which they have been attained. Sometimes two targets a week were set.

LANGUAGE

to say more, on request, when eating bread
to point on request to 'teddy', 'dolly', 'potty', 'sock'
to say/try to say 'car', 'ball', 'dinner', 'dolly', 'shoe', 'cup'
to identify and match (picture/object match) 'shoe' and 'sock'
to find, in book, named picture (bird and house) on request
to reply 'NO' when asked 'Do you want more dinner?'
to say 'YES' on request
to say 'HELLO' on request
to put object ON a surface
to put object UNDER a surface

LANGUAGE/COGNITIVE

to point to herself when asked 'where's Ellen?'
to bring named object (out of three) on request (cruising not walking at that stage)
to identify (via touch or point) two body parts, 'mouth', 'eyes'
to identify on a person 'hair'
to point to own nose on request
to select object from identical array of three (i.e. three balls, or books or teddies)
to make a choice when presented with two objects (parents to ask Ellen to choose)
using mirror, to name parts of her body

SOCIAL AND SELF-HELP

to lift hand and arm unaided on request
to wave arm on request
to take spoon from mouth unaided
to return empty spoon to plate
to pull sock off on request
to pull vest off over shoulders on request
to sit on potty unaided (without pants on) on request
to dry hands unaided on request
to remove coat (with help)

MOTOR

to walk on request, supported by trolley
to walk, holding adult hand, and pushing trolley
to roll a ball along floor
to make a mark on paper
to join up large dots on request with guidance

The histogram (in Figure 2) illustrates Ellen's *approximate* developmental stage and level by the summer of 1985. Within each 'box' it can be seen at a glance the number of items continuously ticked as well as others ticked, therefore attained. Cross-checking

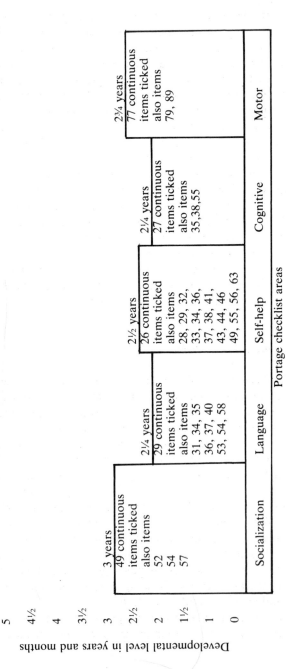

Figure 2: Ellen G. (DB 15.9.1982): Histogram representation of current mastery level covering the period January 1984 to July 1985 by checklist item number and *approximate* developmental age.

with targets achieved will confirm that mastery represents a mix of successful Portage targets and other skills attained outside Portage. This profile also indicates developmental variability, and confirms that in young children development is neither necessarily continuous (smoothly through developmental 'milestones') nor necessarily uniform across developmental and skill areas.

Ellen's profile, represented in this way, shows consistency of skill acquisition and steady progress, yet also highlights those areas that could be priorities for continued assistance, via Portage or other sorts of school and home teaching.

A postscript to this account is that Ellen's new home visitor, Richard Crombie, an MSc educational psychologist trainee, worked with Linda and Chris on targets which were designed to assist Ellen to settle into nursery school, from January 1986. Objectives included self-help and independence skills and prerequisite school skills, for example for eventual drawing, copying, pencil control. This represented a continuing blend of meeting Ellen's then current learning needs as well as anticipating future learning needs within a new context.

Portage and special needs

The final section of this account represents my accumulating experience as a Portage worker, using my contact with Ellen and her parents as a reference point, and drawing upon recent and current work with parents involved in assessment.

There is some evidence that parents' understanding and use of Portage principles and practice aids them in appraising and assessing their children's progress generally. This was confirmed in a small local project carried out by this author and several parents with pre-school Down's syndrome children (Wolfendale, 1984, 1985b). The parents constructed a parental profile of their child, 'My child at home', and it was notable that they were influenced by the developmental areas delineated in the Portage checklist. However they used these as signposts, guidelines which served as a basis to generate their own headings, these being most relevant to their family context, and their child's progress.

The outcomes from this pilot project led to a national pilot and feasibility study into the potential value of providing guidelines for parents, to assist them in contributing their 'parental views' in writing to assessment under section 5 of the 1981 Education Act (Wolfendale, 1985c). The study generated a considerable number of parental contributions and led to a revision of the draft guidelines which were tried out as part of the study (for further details contact this author).

Linda and Chris wrote a parental profile on Ellen, which they submitted as their parental 'evidence' to section 5, and this is reproduced in Appendix I. The written parental contribution provides an opportunity to report upon Portage provision and Portage progress and adds a parental perspective to a home visitor's account.

Concluding comments

The framework and structure of Portage allows for a creative relationship between home visitor and parents on behalf of the child. The adults endorse, monitor and validate each other during the regular (weekly) progress appraisal. Parents' expertise is enhanced by constant dialogue with a professional, whose own credibility is maintained by appointment and promise keeping, and focused attention to task – a stark contrast to the traditional casework practice of random home visits, no specified objectives, and no contract or agreement on how to achieve these. The educational target and goals are paramount; important corollaries to attainment of these are celebrating success, as well as sharing and discussing 'failure' and disappointments.

Portage, as an example of good practice, was referred to several times in the Fish Report (1985) which calls for partnership with parents, of which Portage in the UK is currently the prime model. The Fish Report recommended further 'skills training' for parents and for the professionals who work closely with children and their parents. Again, Portage is an approach which offers 'on the job' skills training, giving plenty of opportunities for practice and skill improvement. Children make tangible progress and parents gain confidence in directly participating in their children's learning.

Appendix I

Parental contribution to statement of special educational needs under section 5(3) of the 1981 Education Act

ELLEN GOODEY

Ellen is two years and two months old. She was diagnosed at birth as having Down's syndrome. When she was four weeks old we were told by a Newham paediatrician that because she was severely mentally handicapped she would be eventually going to a school for severely educationally subnormal children. At the time we did not question this placement, but we have come to do so gradually over a period.

Ellen's motor development has been slow, but with the help of physiotherapy and Portage she walked at 19 months and is now able to climb stairs unaided, walk backwards, and is beginning to run.

She can name a large number of pictures in books and in photographs, both nouns and verbs, and as far as we can tell, her cognitive development is level with that of many two-year-olds who are not severely mentally handicapped.

Her social skills are in advance of what is usually expected from a non-handicapped two-year-old.

Ellen has been able to feed herself and drink from an open cup from the age of 15 months. She asks to go to the toilet. She is clean 90 per cent of the time and dry 50 per cent. She can partly dress and undress herself, imitates drying herself, combing her hair and cleaning her teeth.

Her expressive language is developing at a much slower pace than would usually be expected of a non-handicapped two-year-old. However, she has been learning the Makaton signing vocabulary and uses about 40 signs. She has used more signs, but often drops them when she is able to say the word. She pronounces ten words fully and clearly, and a further 30 incompletely. She will try to say any word which is introduced to her, and has just started to put two words together, usually combining a Makaton sign with a spoken word. At the moment her receptive language skills seem to be a long way ahead of her expressive skills.

Ellen's development so far has led us to the conclusion that it is different from the development of children who are not severely mentally handicapped, and that it is not correct to describe it as 'retarded'. Apart from the area of expressive language, her achievements are similar to those of non-handicapped children of her age. However, the *route* to her achievements has been different, and has required different kinds of input. She does not learn 'automatically', as other children seem to do at this age, and more things have to be taught to her directly or over a longer period of time. But this is balanced by the fact that she is more amenable to teaching than many non-handicapped children.

This is a contribution to Ellen's statement and therefore has the purpose of establishing her learning difficulties. In our view her learning difficulties are only 'difficulties' in the sense that they are different from the common types of difficulty which can occur with most other children.

Ellen's needs are:

1   She needs to learn how to fulfil a role in life both now and after she leaves school, and to be a happy, participating member of her community.

2   She needs to be accepted as a human being with full rights, not someone to be laughed at or feared.

3   She needs to be included in a full range of activities alongside her peers.

4   As a means towards exercising these rights, she needs to develop her physical, communicative, logical, artistic, musical, practical and social skills as far as possible.

None of these needs is special, since they are taken for granted in the case of the vast majority of children. They are only 'special' in Ellen's case because fulfilment of them is usually denied to severely subnormal people, and because she may require more resources in order for them to be met than is usually the case. What is special is the provision needed, and we consider the following special educational provision to be necessary for the time being if Ellen's needs are to be met:

1 Placement in her local neighbourhood school (St Stephens Nursery School), where she will receive the stimulation that she needs from her peers. The authority's normal practice, as revealed to us when Ellen was born, would be to place her in Beckton School nursery class. It is clearly impossible to meet the first three of the above needs if she is segregated from her peers and her local community. Section 2(2) of the 1981 Education Act states that where an authority arranges special educational provision for a child for whom it maintains a statement, it has a duty to secure that he or she is educated in an ordinary school. We can therefore see no grounds for Ellen to be denied the placement we are asking for.

2 The staff who will be in most immediate contact with Ellen need to understand the nature of her condition and the general way in which her development differs from the norm.

3 This staff may need to acquire some knowledge of the Makaton signing vocabulary.

4 This staff will also need to understand how to catch and hold Ellen's attention, and to get used to the speed at which she reacts to events, verbal instructions, etc.

5 There must be extra close liaison between home and school, so that Ellen's time at home can be used to reinforce what she is doing at school.

6 We expect that Ellen will continue to need speech therapy. However, we see no reason why this should not continue to take place under the present arrangements rather than in school.

Note: Ellen has received physiotherapy, speech therapy, occupational therapy and Portage. Those who have worked in these areas with Ellen include Mrs Sandra Holt, Mrs Pauline Barnett, Mrs Pat Kennedy and Mrs Sheila Wolfendale. You may wish to consult them.

Signed: Linda Jordan and Chris Goodey (Ellen's parents)

CHAPTER 3
The Development of Portage in the United Kingdom

John Smith

John Smith was Research Officer for the Wessex Health Care Evaluation Team and is now Deputy Director, Dorchester Cheshire Homes, Dorset.

The word 'Portage' means different things to different people. This is only to be expected as Portage is an educational package comprising several components. There are structural, material and performance components each of which tend to be emphasized at different times and in different settings. Indeed, in the late 1970s, after its initial introduction into the United Kingdom, this confusion was aided and abetted by various misrepresentations in the local and national press. One national nursing journal (now defunct) managed to perpetrate four printing errors in the two short paragraphs of their report, culminating in the appellation 'Postage'.

It was also common in the early days (and still not unknown) for those inhabitants of the British Isles living in southern latitudes, to pronounce the word Portage with the emphasis on the last syllable. For a while I, and my colleagues, assumed this was entirely due to differences in regional accents until we were told on several occasions when addressing audiences that many people had assumed that because the curriculum cards were carried around in a small container, they were portable and therefore the name Portage. It came as something of a letdown when they were told that the name merely reflected the place in Wisconsin where the scheme had originated!

A great deal of confusion (and sometimes later antagonism) was created in the early days by and for those people who bought the checklist and cards and assumed that Portage consisted of a developmental checklist and the associated curriculum cards. Since the box containing the curriculum cards also had a small manual enclosed, few people who bought the materials without attending a presentation or training workshop bothered to buy a handbook entitled *The Portage Guide to Home Teaching* which contained details of (among other things) how to write activity charts. Hence the frequent surprise felt by many of those who thought they had been 'doing' Portage by handing out curriculum cards to parents and expecting them to carry out the activities listed thereon. (This is not to detract from the usefulness of the Portage checklist and curriculum cards in helping many special education teachers to devise a curriculum for some at least of their children.)

Missing parents

It is useful to remind ourselves of this initial, and sometimes continuing, confusion about what Portage is because, after ten years, conditions have changed and we tend to forget what was (or rather was not) available for families with a pre-school mentally handicapped child. One of the most striking features of the literature on mental handicap prior to the late 1960s is the scarcity of the mention of parents. Even when parents did begin to be included in descriptions of surveys the emphasis was on the effect the handicapped member had on the rest of the family. This was no doubt due in part to the interests and skills of researchers conducting studies involving families with a disabled member whether mentally ill, elderly, mentally handicapped, etc. The main thrust in looking at such families at that time was concentrated on establishing the degree of 'family burden' and one of the main objectives of such studies was to devise valid and reliable measures of family burden. Objective measures looked at the disruption to household and family life whilst attempts were made to design subjective measures of the personal feelings of family members of carrying a burden, being distressed, unhappy, upset, etc. This was the approach used by Tizard and Grad (1961) in their Middlesex survey. Although producing useful information, there is no evidence that parents were looked on as possible agents of change for their own children. There is evidence that there was only a slow change in the way parents were perceived; the survey carried out for the Warnock Committee found that whether parents with a pre-school handicapped child received educational counselling depended largely on whether the child was going to attend some form of day provision before age five (Laing, 1979).

Surveys carried out in the late 1960s and early 1970s revealed that the professionals who had contact with families reported that parents experienced major problems because they felt unable to assist their child in the development of new appropriate skills or to overcome behaviour problems (Hewett, 1970). The parents themselves reported that they welcomed contact with the professionals who were generally kind and generous but were unable to help the parents teach specific skills (Fox, 1973; Lloyd-Bostock, 1976).

Parental involvement

It was during the late 1950s and early 1960s that important advances were made (mainly in the USA) in the application of behavioural methods, originally developed in laboratory-type settings, to the teaching of new skills to children and to the decrease of their difficult behaviours (Bijou, 1955,1957,1961; Ferster and De Meyer, 1961). Later these methods (behaviour modification and precision teaching) were taught to teachers in schools and to parents to carry out in their own homes (Wahler *et al.*, 1965; Wolf *et al.*, 1964; Risley and Wolf, 1967). The methods were gradually introduced into the UK by professionals with individual cases – primarily psychologists and psychiatrists in university departments.

These experts then began to look for means to disseminate and apply these methods more widely. One obvious way which was utilized was to include the teaching of behaviour modification skills on the curricula of a wide range of professional courses – nurses, teachers, social workers, etc. Another was to introduce parents themselves to the application of these methods.

Most of the early teaching of parents was via their regular attendance at a once-weekly evening group workshop. This was usually divided into two parts, the first being didactic (usually an illustrated lecture on a particular principal topic), the second usually consisting of tutor-led group discussions about particular parental problems, including discussion between parents themselves (Cunningham and Jeffree, 1971; Callias and Jenkins,

1973; Bidder *et al.*, 1975). Although these studies showed that parents could teach their handicapped child to acquire new skills and/or to lose problem behaviour this model of parental group workshop was found to have a number of drawbacks. The parents were self-selected, therefore well motivated and tended to have ready access to baby-sitting and cars. Thus there tended to be few families from social classes 4 and 5. Also, the interventions were mainly devised at the workshops which were not attended by the children.

A detailed evaluation of one group programme (Watson and Bassinger, 1974) showed that although theoretical skills could be acquired by parents at a group workshop – measured by pencil and paper tests – this did not necessarily lead to their implementing teaching procedures with their children. More success at helping parents to continue teaching programmes at home was achieved with autistic children by Howlin *et al.* (1973) when parents were visited at home by one professional as well as initially attending a clinic.

In the late 1960s Tharp and Wetzel (1969) had developed and evaluated what they called the 'triadic' model in order to deliver a service to delinquent youths. In this model an intermediate 'level' of personnel was introduced between the highly skilled professionals and the parents. These 'behavior analysts' were trained by the professionals in a short time to teach the parents and others to set and attain limited objectives with the youths in the places where they spent their day (home, school, etc.). Records on the goals set and attained formed the basis of a detailed monitoring procedure which contributed greatly to the satisfactory maintenance of the performances at all levels of the service.

A similar model (Portage) was adopted by David Shearer when he was asked to help set up a service for pre-school handicapped children in south-central, rural Wisconsin. Originally it had been intended to provide a central class which the children would attend but due to the sparsely populated region the service had to be home based which meant that the parents were the direct teachers. They were visited weekly by 'home teachers' who in turn reported weekly to a 'supervisor' on all the homes they visited. Later work at Portage demonstrated that it was possible to train 'home teachers' with a variety of backgrounds quickly and successfully with results similar to those attained by teachers with professional qualifications (Schortinghuis and Frohman, 1974).

Early UK initiatives

In the United Kingdom in the mid-1970s there was an increasing demand for assistance by parents wishing to help their handicapped children to acquire skills and to lose disruptive behaviours. During a visit to the USA in 1974 Albert Kushlick, Director of the Wessex Health Care Evaluation Research Team, mentioned the position in the UK to Professor Sidney Bijou who wholeheartedly recommended the Portage project as a model which had not only been successfully demonstrated but was also one of the few early education schemes funded by the Bureau of Education for the Handicapped to receive repeated funding and a recommendation that it become a model project for replication in other parts of the USA.

As a result a demonstration project was set up in Wessex (Smith *et al.*, 1977). A similar interest had been shown in developing a home teaching service in South Wales and in May and June, 1976, three 3-day training workshops (two in Hampshire and one in Cardiff) were run by George Jesien and Betsy May from the parent project in Wisconsin. As well as the people who were to make up the services in Wessex and Cardiff, people attended from several parts of the UK, although numbers were limited to ensure adequate training. Several of those who attended were able to go away and set up a Portage home teaching service in their own locality.

The 1976 workshops (as do current initial workshops) concentrated on the basic skills required by home teachers in order to prepare well-written activity charts. Precision teaching is a format for devising and monitoring educational interventions (although the same method is applicable to goals other than educational ones). The actual content of the intervention is left up to the inclination of teacher and parents. The only restriction is that interventions are observable and therefore measurable and so monitorable.

One of the main benefits of these workshops was the obvious enthusiasm of the trainers and the emphasis on being positive. For example when asked (as home teachers often are) 'where do I start with someone short on motivation' by a concerned attender, George Jesien responded 'start where they are at'. The attender's response to this was 'but she spends most of her time lying on the settee, watching TV and eating chocolates'. George replied 'then the initial objective will be to design an intervention which the mother can carry out with the child whilst lying on the settee watching TV and eating chocolates'. It is amazing how often highly qualified professionals still complain that they cannot get parents to implement a programme without realizing that the goals they are setting are far too ambitious – i.e. the *distance* between what the parents can do now and what the professional wishes them to do is too great.

The axiom 'tiny steps for tiny people' was devised to apply to children but the principle applies equally to all settings and all people. One of the components of Portage is that the 'home teacher' will demonstrate, in front of a parent, what it is that the teacher is recommending the parent to do during the next week and then watch the parent doing it. This provides immediate feedback as to whether the parent can in fact do the activity and gives confidence to carry on doing it for the remainder of the week. In this way the home teacher can ensure that the parent is not being asked to do too much or attempt something which is too difficult. It also removes the opportunity for the 'professional' to complain that parents cannot follow their suggestions. By seeing that parents have been able to carry out suggested activities before they have left the home, Portage teachers have been able to ensure that 'teaching is doomed to success'. This approach helps professionals to operationalize one element of the concept of accountability in that if they were to give activities which parents were unable to carry out they would be *giving parents problems* instead of *helping them solve problems*. Of course even watching the parent does not remove the possibility that for one reason or another the child fails to attain the goal set. Here again an essential part of the home teacher's repertoire is to take the blame for the lack of success and to emphasize that either the step set for the child to acquire was too large or that the method the teacher had devised was inappropriate (or not good enough or whatever).

The Wessex study

The Wessex Portage project built on the developments of the Wisconsin Portage project which had demonstrated that home teacher performances could be carried out by paraprofessionals as well as trained teachers (Schortinghuis and Frohman, *op. cit.*). In Wessex there were three home teachers, only one of whom was a trained teacher – the others were a health visitor and a family service worker. Whereas in Wisconsin where Portage had been (and is) run by one agency – education – and in South Glamorgan where the home teaching service was run by health, in Wessex the opportunity was taken to develop a multi-agency service. Not only did the three home teachers belong to different agencies (health, social services and education) but they were supervised by someone from another profession – an educational psychologist. This was partly done to test the feasibility of jointly implementing services to families with pre-school children as recommended for example by the Warnock Report (1978). The evaluation of the Wessex project (Smith *et al., op. cit.*) and the continuing success of the Winchester Portage service (as well as other multi-agency services in the UK) has demonstrated the success of joint service provision. Unfortunately such provision is still in a minority of the Portage services set up in the UK (Bendall *et al.*, 1984).

The Wessex project demonstrated that children, parents and home teachers were able to attain the objectives set for them. The home teachers were able to visit families weekly and to carry out the procedures within the 1½ hours allocated. Many commentators complain of the difficulty of providing home-based services because they can never find the parents at home when they call – in Wessex and most other Portage services home teachers visit homes at the same time and on the same day each week, unless there is an agreed change due to holiday, illness, etc. In Wessex one parent insisted on carrying on with the teaching activities whilst on a camping holiday during which there were several mishaps including the death of an elderly relative and the apprehension of another by the police! Families also carried out activities when the home teacher was on holiday.

The data from activity charts showed that home teachers set activities in all areas of the curriculum including areas where a child was particularly delayed. 80 per cent of goals set were attained within the week or when the home teacher next visited (i.e. after one week). Later data from the activity charts showed that the success rate went up to 90 per cent and 95 per cent and this was maintained after the end of the research project when the Wessex project became two services – Winchester Portage service and Basingstoke Portage service.

Over a six-month period parents in the Wessex project carried out over 2000 teaching trials. It is often necessary to remind people who have not been involved in Portage that most parents spend only a few minutes each day on specific Portage activities as each teaching trial usually takes seconds rather than minutes, e.g. helping a child to lift its head, or to draw a circle or name a member of the family. The emphasis is always to fit activities into the way of life of the family according to the skill repertoire of the child.

Consumer response

The Wessex project asked parents for their opinions of the service and to answer questions specifically related to what the home teachers did. The parents said that they were regularly consulted about which area of the curriculum they wanted to work with their child and that teachers always demonstrated the activities they suggested and ensured parents could carry them out before they left the home. Parents were not concerned that their other children (if they had any) might be excluded due to any additional commitment required of them in carrying out the activities – in many families home teachers involved the other children in some way or gave them their own activities to be attained by the next week. In at least one family it was not just the children who benefited from the visits of the home teacher. There is for example the famous story of the table-tennis ball. One mother apologetically mentioned to a home teacher that although her young son could now take himself to the toilet when he needed to micturate, and could dress and undress himself, his aim was not very good so that he frequently wet the floor on either side of the toilet-bowl. The home teacher thereupon produced a table-tennis ball, which of course does not flush away, and painted a red spot on the ball. She then drew up an activity chart; the teaching objective was that the boy would hit the red spot on the ball with his stream of urine and mother would record the frequency with which he missed the bowl. At the home teacher's next visit the mother excitedly met her at the door and when asked how the activity had gone the mother said that not only was her son now able to aim correctly 100 per cent of the time, but her husband was too!

Individualized teaching

One of the earliest misapprehensions about Portage was that, because there was a checklist containing several hundred behaviours, for each of which there was a curriculum card containing suggestions as to how that behaviour might be taught, the programmes were fixed and were in some sort of predetermined sequence. In fact the opposite is the case, in that, because every child is different, the use of the checklist enables the parents and teacher to establish the behaviours the child already has and then to *select* which skills to teach next. Skilful teachers rarely need to refer to the curriculum cards and in the first six months of the Wessex project parents and teachers rapidly learned to devise their own activities. Great use was, and is, made of the skills of professionals such as occupational, speech and physiotherapists, as well as specialist teachers for the deaf, blind, etc. Similarly, because the steps on the Portage checklist can rarely be attained within a week parents and teachers quickly become adept at task analysis. Indeed one of the major factors in the successful maintenance of parents continuing to carry out three or four activities each week for two, three or more years is that the teaching targets set are attained with over 90 per cent success rate. And these are meaningful teaching targets. Critics who have mentioned that possibly the steps attained are negligible or meaningless have obviously never been closely involved in a weekly home visiting service where parents are encouraged to be the major partners. In this sort of relationship parents are quick to point out deficiencies – although they also quickly get into the swing of positively reinforcing the visiting home teacher as well as the child.

The Wessex project, then, demonstrated that the children gained skills, the parents were able to carry out the teaching and the teachers were able to do regular visits and to teach the parents. In addition these performances of children, parents and teachers could be regularly and positively monitored by a supervisor (educational psychologist) who reported to a multi-disciplinary multi-agency management team comprising professionals and managers from health, social services, education and voluntary agencies, as well as parents. The Portage-type home visiting service in South Glamorgan which began at about the same time (Revill and Blunden, 1979a; Barna *et al.*, 1980) demonstrated that children receiving Portage made more progress than when they did not receive Portage. However there was variation between children as to the amount of progress made. This had been noticed in Wessex too and is mainly due to the initial differences between children (a multiply handicapped child clearly has fewer skills than does an able child with Down's syndrome). It is therefore only to be expected that there will be differential rates of progress.

To parents this is not a major problem as those with very severely retarded children are well aware of their child's limited skills and rarely, if ever, are expecting miraculous progress. What they do want to see, and what they get and can see with Portage is regular, constant weekly attainment through appropriate goals being specifically set for their child – i.e. they are geared to success as measured by weekly activity charts and are not into measuring success by the large steps entered on Portage or other developmental checklists.

In the early days in Winchester one of the most heartwarming reports on the useful effects of Portage was given by the mother of a very severely physically and mentally handicapped child who in addition had family and social problems. She said that when she felt overwhelmed by all the troubles in her life the one ray of sunshine was provided for her by looking at her son's activity chart because there she could see, from the ticks, that something had been achieved and this gave her added confidence to continue facing the other difficulties in her life. It is this regular, positive feedback that helps parents to continue with what is often a very difficult and arduous daily life.

Teaching materials

It was soon realized in Wessex and South Wales (and no doubt in other areas) that the language and communication section of the Portage curriculum was the least satisfactory of the six broad areas of the *Portage Guide to Early Education*. Over the period of the next few years this section was re-vamped using the same principles as had been employed in Wisconsin – i.e. for each behavioural step identified a number of activities were devised. Indeed, certainly in Wessex, a veto was put on new steps unless activities had been not only devised, but successfully implemented. In addition many language items were contained in other sections of the Portage curriculum – especially socialization. In their revision of this section, the *Wessex Revised Portage Language Checklist,* White and East (1983) drew people's attention to the speech items in other sections as well as adding additional items and activities. This has been a most useful addition as parents are usually particularly keen to work on the early stages of speech with their child and this is widely recognized as being one of the most difficult areas to teach.

The Portage materials were soon adopted by teachers and others working with people who had a wide variety of skill deficits. This prompted teachers, psychologists and others to supplement and/or adjust the basic Portage checklist and curriculum. Thus at one end of the scale a checklist and curriculum were developed and evaluated for use with multiply handicapped children (Dessent and Ferguson, 1984) and at the other end of the scale additional items were developed for severely retarded adults (Jenkins *et al.,* 1983).

The spread of Portage

As a result of talks by the Wessex Portage team and others at local, national and international public meetings great interest was aroused in other parts of the United Kingdom which often led to the establishment and evaluation of similar home teaching services (e.g. Cusworth, 1980; Daly, 1980). These evaluations demonstrated that the Portage service as developed in Wessex could be replicated in other parts of the country with similarly excellent results. Similarly, replications of the service in South Glamorgan were carried out in other parts of Wales (Holland and Noaks, 1982; Jones *et al.,* 1979).

An added impetus was given to the spread of Portage services throughout this country by the 'second wave' of workshops given here by staff from Wisconsin. These followed a visit to Portage, Wisconsin, by Vince Gorman, the Director of Nursing Services at Northgate Hospital in Northumberland. He arranged for two Portage staff members, Dick Boyd and Susie Frohman, to present a number of two-day workshops during two weeks in June 1979. Some 270 people attended these workshops. A similar series of workshops was carried out in 1980 by Wisconsin staff. For the last six years, twice-yearly workshops have been given in Hampshire, organized by R.J. Cameron and Mollie White, using home teachers and (most usefully) parents as a major part of the course. The National Portage Association also runs basic Portage workshops.

In August 1981, the First National Portage Conference was held in Lymington, Hampshire. This attracted attenders from all over the United Kingdom and highlighted the many different settings and structures in which Portage had developed. One young lady was extremely pleased to be able to meet and talk to others using Portage as she herself provided, alone, a home teaching service to an enormous area of Scotland and the Western Isles! The Conference provided (and its successors continue to provide) an extremely reinforcing setting for all those involved with Portage. Indeed it is now so popular that numbers have to be limited and as many people have to be turned down as eventually attend. It is also very gratifying to see the large numbers of parents who attend and make major contributions by presentations and discussions. This ensures that the object of the whole exercise does not get lost in a welter of theory and jargon.

The National Survey

In 1982–83 the Wessex Health Care Evaluation Research Team conducted a National Portage Survey (Bendall *et al.*, 1984) in order to assess the extent to which Portage had been replicated in the United Kingdom. In order to make this study manageable it was necessary to set criteria for which services would be included in the survey. It was already evident from the report of the First National Portage Conference (Cameron, 1982) that Portage had been implemented in many settings other than the family home – e.g. hospitals, children's homes, paediatric units, opportunity playgroups, etc. – and using people other than parents as the 'direct teachers'. Therefore information was collected on 'Portage-type'* home teaching services in relation to the following seven criteria:

1 Families were regularly visited in their own homes.
2 Assessment included the use of a developmental checklist.

---

* The term 'Portage-type' was used in order to include services which met all seven criteria but did not call themselves 'Portage'.

3 Written instructions for teaching and recording were given to parents.
4 The suggested teaching procedure was modelled for the parent(s).
5 The parent was observed carrying out the teaching procedure and recording.
6 Baseline and post-baseline data were recorded.
7 Home visitors attended a regular staff meeting.

The term parent also covered foster-parent or someone in the home (e.g. another relative) who was carrying out parent-type duties. Requests for information were sent out to all health, social service, education and relevant voluntary agencies in the United Kingdom as well as to specific individuals. Of the 616 agencies and individuals who were approached 567 (92 per cent) replied identifying 221 services of which 130 (58 per cent) satisfied all seven criteria. Of the services which did not meet all criteria, 24 were not home visiting, 14 did not use written instructions, 33 comprised single individuals working alone (and hence did not have regular staff meetings), three did not model the teaching procedure and the rest, although they did home visits, wrote instructions, had regular staff meetings and modelled teaching procedures, did not meet one or more of the other criteria.

Whereas the Portage service in Wisconsin was developed to serve a widely spread, sparse population, the National Portage Survey revealed a concentration of services in the large conurbations and hence there was an absence of Portage services in the rural, sparsely populated areas.

The majority of the 130 Portage-type home teaching services catered only for pre-school children and all served mentally handicapped clients. Some included physically handicapped clients but only a few took clients who were only sensorily impaired, or were abused or categorized only as behaviour/management problems.

More detailed information was collected on 59 continuing Portage-type services. Of these 23 were provided jointly by health, social services and education, 19 were single agency (13 health, four education and two social services) and five were funded by voluntary agencies. In addition, ten services had one home teacher – they also had a supervisor, and two services had unpaid home teachers who worked in their own time. A wide variety of professionals (and parents) were working as home teachers thus reinforcing the finding in Wessex that with positive monitoring it is possible to make use of people from a wide range of backgrounds. This has obviously aided the rapid dissemination. However this does not mean that there is no necessity for continuing to set the occasion for home teachers to take aboard new ideas, teaching techniques, etc. Many services include a presentation or training session as part of their regular staff meetings.

Only 5 per cent of the services reported that on average home teachers left more than two activity charts per family at each home visit. There is no evidence from this that parents are being asked to spend an exorbitant amount of time on Portage activities to the exclusion of other matters. These data fit in well with the Portage policy of being easily accommodated in the family setting. 94 per cent of parents thought they were asked to do about the right number of activities and none thought they were asked to do too many. 64 per cent of parents said they did the activities every day and a further 35 per cent said they did the activities most days. 30 per cent of parents spent less than 15 minutes per day on activities, 54 per cent spent between 15 and 30 minutes per day on activities. 96 per cent of parents said they were able to follow the directions on activity charts and to keep records. 20 per cent of families where there was a husband or other adult male reported that the male always carried out activities with the child, 42 per cent said the male sometimes did, 21 per cent said that the male did not carry out activities very often and 17 per cent said that the male never did. 32 per cent of males said they would like to be more involved, 66 per cent were happy with their current involvement and only one said he would like to be less involved.

65 per cent of services had five or less home teachers and 85 per cent of all home teachers worked less than ten hours per week on Portage. 91 per cent of home teachers had other employment and of these 19 per cent were health visitors, 12 per cent teachers, 12 per cent social workers and 10 per cent community mental handicap nurses. Other home teachers were psychologists, nursery nurses, occupational therapists, physiotherapists and speech therapists. 17 per cent of services had home teachers who were parents of a mentally handicapped child – one service having four such. 76 per cent of home teachers visited three families or less.

65 per cent of services had no special funding – the staff were either carrying out their Portage activities within their normal caseload or were unpaid, 16 per cent had special funding from statutory agencies and the rest obtained their funds from other sources – usually voluntary agencies.

Over one-third of services reported that they had carried out no form of evaluation or done a pilot study.

In general one can conclude that within six years there had been a massive change throughout the UK in the provision available to families with a pre-school mentally handicapped child. This had been largely provided through replicating the major components of the Portage model and the majority of services were being successfully maintained. However this does not mean that they were static. Most services were changing as they developed, although keeping within the criteria generally agreed as defining Portage.

The National Portage Survey was mainly restricted to home teaching services. There have been major spin-offs from Portage in schools, residential and other facilities attended by mentally handicapped and also in settings attended by people with a wide range of disabilities.

At the 1982 National Portage Conference there was a meeting of those interested in establishing a National Portage Association (Kushlick, 1984). An ad hoc committee met regularly during the next year in order to draw up the remit of the Association. This was adopted and committee members were elected at the Third Portage Conference in 1983. The NPA has rapidly become a useful addition for the promotion and regulation of Portage services. The work of the National Portage Association is described elsewhere in this volume. It was extremely influential in persuading the Department of Education and Science that for three years Portage should be included in the educational support grant scheme whereby local education authorities apply for earmarked money. One of their most remarkable successes in this respect was to persuade the DES that such money should be used to support multi-agency projects and was not just available to education authorities as is usually the case with ESG monies. One of the useful functions of the National Portage Association is that in acting as a registration body for those who wish to be considered as Portage services, help and advice is readily available to those wishing to set up Portage services.

In conclusion, it is possible to say that in ten years Portage has made a tremendous impact on services for handicapped people and their families – especially on families with a pre-school child. It has clearly filled an obvious gap in the service system and has contributed much to the cause of involving parents as real partners in the education and care of their children.

CHAPTER 4
Sharing Expertise: Portage into Schools Will Go!

Robert J. Cameron

Although originally designed as a home teaching programme which aimed to teach parents to work effectively with their children who had special needs, the assets of the Portage home teaching model were soon appreciated by staff working in school and other centre-based settings.

Not surprisingly, in the early years, the more tangible features of the Portage model were the first to be spotted by teachers. The Portage checklist, one of the most detailed available, was seen as a useful skill assessment tool, particularly by teachers working with mildly and severely handicapped pupils. On the other hand, it would be correct to say that the Portage teaching cards frequently attracted disparaging comments from teachers. In retrospect, this was only to be expected since the teaching suggestions they contained were of the simple, low technology variety which could be used by parents in a home setting. Needless to say, most experienced teachers could suggest more 'professional methods' of attaining similar objectives.

For most schools in the mid-1970s the phrase 'doing Portage' meant that the Portage checklist was being used as an individualized assessment procedure. However, some teachers had also discovered the Portage basic training workshops. It must be remembered that when the Portage scheme was first introduced into the United Kingdom, a mere six years had elapsed since pupils who had severe learning difficulties were deemed 'educable' and brought into the educational fold by the 1970 Education (Handicapped Children) Act. By the time the first Portage workshops began, most teachers working in special schools had discovered that a watered-down version of a normal school curriculum or a scaled-down modification of 'discovery' teaching methods were less than appropriate for children who had severe learning difficulties.

The dilemma was most dramatically highlighted within the pre-school playgroup movement where Opportunity Playgroups for handicapped children and their siblings were being set up. While most playgroups began with the conviction that all pre-school children learned through play and believed this maxim should apply equally to handicapped children, a large gap between theory and reality immediately became obvious. Clark and Cameron (1983) summarized the problem as follows: 'we soon learnt that handicapped children frequently have to be *taught* to play. Therefore we would have to examine more closely what we hoped they would learn. In other words, play had to be planned!' .

Many components of the Portage workshop were rapidly snapped up and adapted by teachers whose training had often left them ill-equipped to deal with the everyday problems of children in special schools. Particular workshop components, e.g. planning long- and short-term curriculum objectives, reinforcement techniques, correction/teaching procedures, daily practice and fluency building, and detailed ongoing recording procedures, were soon pressed into service in classrooms.

McBride and Gant (1982) concluded that the usefulness of the Portage model lay in its 'comparative simplicity to teach large groups of people such as teachers' and before going on to describe some of the creative adaptations of Portage it is worth highlighting the major features of the successful Portage home teaching model (Daly, 1985; National Portage Association, 1985).

1 Families are visited weekly at home by a visitor who has completed a Portage workshop training course.
2 The Portage home visitor attends a regular staff meeting with the Portage supervisor (and other home visitors).
3 A Portage checklist is used for initial and ongoing assessment.
4 A Portage activity chart, consisting of instructions agreed with the parents on what to teach, how to teach it, what to record, is left with parents each week for each of the skills being taught.
5 The agreed teaching procedures are demonstrated by the home teacher.

6   The home visitor observes the parents carrying out the procedure and offers advice and/or amendments if necessary.
7   The child's level of skill in the area concerned is recorded both before teaching and a week after teaching so that improvements can be measured.
8   There is a management team of representatives from health, social services, education, voluntary agencies and parents which meets every three or four months to receive a supervisor's report and deals with related inter-agency or resource issues.

This formula has proved remarkably successful in helping parents who have children with special needs to teach their children in a *home* setting and as a result the Portage home teaching model has been widely utilized throughout the British Isles.

The trouble with school . . .

When adapting the Portage home teaching model for use in a school setting there are of course a number of important differences which need to be taken into consideration. In the first place, schools (unlike families) are *very large organizations* catering for large numbers of children in a system where a number of different teachers may be involved in teaching a child at different periods of the day or week.

Secondly, while small organizations like families often resist change, larger institutions like schools have even more effective strategies which *work against change* (even if it is for the better). Frederickson and Haran (1986) have reminded us how difficult it can be to overcome this status quo phenomenon which operates in institutions. In this study, the objective was to introduce the Portage model to teachers and nursery nurses working in a day nursery. Although some staff were able to attain this objective, others did not and the features of school organization which prevented them being able to carry out Portage activities included: not being able to find time during the working day to write activity charts, staffing levels being insufficient to free staff to work with individuals on a regular basis and the general time-consuming nature of intensive precision teaching. As well as overcoming these visible institutional problems, Portage may also have to cope with less obvious stereotyped attitudes of teachers to parents, which may become apparent when teachers are asked to drop professional mystiques and share the teaching process.

Finally there is the problem of maintaining *continuity*. In a school the amount of disruption to daily routine which occurs is quite considerable, e.g. sports days, concerts, assemblies, illness of staff, illness of children, etc. Any combination of these can sabotage even the most carefully designed teaching programme.

To minimize the effect of all these difficulties, it is necessary to create a built-in monitoring/management system within the school which aids effective communication, encourages staff to cooperate and share ideas and ensures that the necessary resources (both people and materials) are available.

Advantages for schools

If some of these difficulties can be overcome, then the advantages of a Portage model for schools, staff and the pupils are considerable and include the following:

1 Most successful teaching programmes (as Bronfenbrenner (1974) has reminded us) have a 'parental involvement' component.
2 Parents are likely to take a more positive view of the school.
3 The Portage model in school can encourage positive organizational change, e.g. reassessment of staff attitudes, improved curriculum management, agreed strategies for tackling whole-school problems, etc. In short, Portage can bring about an 'organizational spring clean'.
4 Teachers can share the selection, teaching, assessment and evaluation of curriculum objectives for children with special needs and avoid the all too common isolation of their own classrooms.
5 A Portage management team could offer important new managerial roles to the headteacher, deputy and senior school staff.
6 This type of intervention offers schools the possibility of tackling individual pupil problems of learning and behaviour management before they become intractable (i.e. it is *pre-emptive* not *reactive*).

7   The role specification which exists in Portage, e.g. management team, supervisor, teacher, parent, can help to avoid the all-too-frequently reported phenomenon by teachers of 'feeling undervalued' or 'talked down to'. Roles are not only clearly specified, but each person can see that everyone is making a crucial contribution to the teaching programme.

8   Visiting support professionals (e.g. educational psychologists, advisers, community medical officers, etc.) can be given an *indirect monitoring* role and this may maximize the use of what are usually scarce professional services.

As well as listing mutual advantages of the Portage model in a school setting, it is worth noting that there are a number of arguments which highlight the *unique* suitability of schools for setting up a Portage scheme. Schools are already supported by multi-agency teams and these can be used as a basis for a multi-professional Portage service. It must also be said that teachers per se do have a vital contribution to make to any Portage team and should be regarded as core team members. Finally 'teaching' occupies a central role in Portage, and schools possess specialist expertise, resources and equipment which are specifically designed to aid teaching.

Portage in schools

Given the potential of a Portage model for use within a school setting, it is scarcely surprising that a wide variety of adaptations exist. These schemes tend to fall under two major headings:

(a)   The Portage *teaching* model
      The Behavioural Checklist can be used as a basis of a curriculum planning exercise within the school and activity charts can be adapted for teaching priority objectives in both a home and classroom setting.

(b)   The Portage *service* model
      The Portage model of service delivery can be used to improve home–school liaison or as a multi-agency school-

based home visiting service or as a school 'outreach' facility for staff in neighbouring schools.

Curriculum planning and Portage

Teachers who are concerned with the selection of curriculum objectives for children with special needs either in a special school or mainstream setting have recognized that different levels of *specificity* in curriculum planning are needed. Most curricula in mainstream schools are written in fairly general *teacher management objectives* and these broad statements of teacher intent usually need to be rewritten in precise *pupil objectives* before they can be used successfully by teachers of pupils with moderate or severe learning difficulties. A detailed description of the different levels of curriculum planning is available in Cameron (1981) or Lister and Cameron (1986) where the necessity to use finely grained objectives for pupils who have special educational needs is highlighted.

Writing detailed curriculum objectives for such pupils can be a time and energy consuming exercise. Fortunately, the Portage checklist can be used as a starting point for a core curriculum in schools and this process was used in a curriculum planning project at Cold East Hospital School near Southampton (reported in Cameron, 1979).

More recently, Brosnan and Huggett (1984) described a curriculum management project at the Willows Nursery School in Portsmouth. Each pupil had three teaching targets allocated weekly and these short-term objectives were usually selected for items in the cognitive and motor sections of the Portage checklist (language objectives were taken from the Derbyshire Language Scheme). A large number of the Portage items taught at the Willows had been sequenced (*cf.* Gardner, 1980) so that the pupils were taught sub-skills which directly prepared them for longer term objectives in later schooling.

As is often the case, some of the gaps between items in the teaching programme were very large and necessitated task analysis to break them down into more manageable steps. At the Willows, each time a task analysis was carried out, it was filed away in a filing system (which all school staff shared) where these small steps in a wider teaching programme could be revised and updated 'in the light of teaching experience' (Brosnan and Huggett, *op. cit.*).

The staff at the Willows Nursery went on to develop a more ambitious project which was described as a 'marriage between two major developments in special education: Portage and micro-computers' (Palmer and Huggett, 1985). The Willows micro programme was required to:

1   Keep details of curriculum items and task analyses of items.

2   Keep records of each child under
   (a)   items already achieved
   (b)   items set as long-term targets
   (c)   items set as short-term targets

3   Allow teachers to record the results of teaching present short-term targets and set new targets for the future.

4   Produce activity charts for present short-term targets.

5   Provide summary information on the performance of both individual children and the curriculum as a whole.

When listing the assets and deficits of this unusual project, it was concluded that the approach could be applied in any school setting and the curriculum content was not merely limited to the Portage materials but 'the system would be applicable to any special needs curriculum that is specified in terms of precise objectives' (Palmer and Huggett, *op. cit.*).

At Whitefield School, Walthamstow, the Portage checklist was used to clarify priorities for children with special educational needs (McBride and Gant, 1982) and at Heltwate School, Peterborough, additional items were added to produce a checklist for multiply handicapped children (Dessent and Ferguson, 1984).

All these studies demonstrate that the Portage checklist can be used as a starting point for change within a school system. It is scarcely surprising therefore that Stratford and Coyne (1986) recognizing that Portage can act as a catalyst for change within a school, recommend that a Portage workshop and follow-up curriculum planning and teaching activities should precede the introduction of the 'heavier' behavioural technology of the Education of the Developmentally Young approach (Foxen and McBrien, 1981) which is designed more specifically for severely and multiply handicapped pupils. Portage in this case was seen as a 'gentle introduction to the behavioural technology' (Stratford and Coyne, *op. cit.*).

Teaching method and Portage

The Portage *teaching* process has also been adapted for use in school. In most instances, this has usually meant that objectives in priority need areas have been selected for individual children, activity charts have been used to teach priority objectives and a small positive monitoring team (usually consisting of headteacher and visiting support professionals) has been set up to monitor the scheme.

A good example of this model in action was reported by Dyer and Huggett (1984). At Cedar School for physically handicapped children near Southampton, a class chart was drawn up so that the progress of the nursery class could be monitored on the five Portage developmental areas. At the beginning of each week, the class teacher spent one hour making out activity charts for teaching targets for four priority children in the class. As well as teaching objectives, *maintenance activities* for the teaching targets adopted for that week were identified since 'this offered opportunities for skills learnt in a more formalized teaching setting to be generalized and maintained'. One special feature of the Cedar School project (monitored by a visiting educational psychologist) was that equipment within the classroom was classified in terms of Portage checklist items so that maintenance activities could be listed under the appropriate checklist item.

A similar scheme has operated for the past three years at Mordaunt School, Southampton. This is a school where the pupils have severe learning and physical difficulties. Apart from Portage activity charts being used to teach priority objectives to children throughout the school, an interesting addition was that of a management team (headteacher, two visiting psychologists and three parents) which meets on a six-monthly basis. It is gratifying to be able to report at the time of writing that although considerable changes have occurred in the senior management of the school, the project continues almost unaltered (personal communication).

The need for structured teaching of children with special needs has been frequently highlighted (see especially Ainscow and Tweddle, 1979; Becker *et al.*, 1981; Faupel and Cameron, 1984), yet it has also been recognized that highly structured teaching is not only hard work but can be sometimes uneconomical (especially in terms of teacher time and effort). The need to match teaching method to pupil need has been highlighted (Faupel, 1986) and some consideration may have to be given to the use of ancillary help, e.g. classroom aides or parents. The latter may need to be used as direct contact teaching personnel while the class teacher's expertise could be used in the indirect but equally vital tasks of selecting objectives, writing activity charts and monitoring the work of classroom helpers.

Home–school liaison and Portage

Bridging the geographical and professional gap between what happens to any child at home and at school has proved to be a formidable task for most schools. Strategies for improving home–school liaison range from end of term reports to parents' evenings and home–school notebooks, all of which have serious limitations. Parent-teacher contact is important for all pupils, and in the case of the special needs child such liaison is vital for continuity of learning. A number of schools have adapted the Portage service model as a means of ensuring close parent-teacher cooperation.

Although the Portage checklist was originally introduced to ascertain the existing repertoire of pupils at Icknield School, Andover, and to plan their future teaching activities, staff were also able to use these data to involve parents in the teaching process by means of one-a-month 'parent involvement days' (Cameron, 1979).

A similar scheme at Whitefield School, Walthamstow, was reported by McBride and Gant (*op. cit.*). In this case, parents could come into school for a weekly meeting. Here the class teacher was able to describe the teaching objective which was being carried out in the classroom, demonstrate with the child present and then observe the parents' trying out this teaching procedure. At each weekly meeting, parents reported on the previous week's teaching

task and handed in a completed activity chart for discussion.
It may not always be possible for parents to visit school regularly, especially if, as Dyer and Huggett (1984) remind us, 'families can live anything up to 25 miles from the school and often the child is brought in by prearranged transport each day'. In such cases, a written activity chart can provide a detailed description of school activities which parents can continue in the home setting. Such continuity ensures that the pupil receives additional practice (*fluency building*) as well as opportunities to *generalize* learned skills to settings other than the classroom, particularly those home and community contexts in which most time is spent.

Portage home visiting and schools

Parental involvement schemes have been one of the growth phenomena of the 1980s and the success of shared and paired schemes in particular is well documented (see Topping and Wolfendale (1985) for an overview of such projects). Unlike home–school liaison approaches which seek to ensure that work in school is supplemented by supporting activities at home, parental involvement projects have viewed the home as an important learning environment in its own right and attempted systematically to involve parents in teaching basic skills like reading. Some special schools have used the Portage model as a medium for supplementing parent teaching skills by providing a home visiting service.

Such a home visiting service for several families whose children attended Medecroft Opportunity Centre, Winchester, was reported by Cameron (1979). This service was originally introduced to combat those problems which parents reported at home but which occurred rarely if ever in a school setting. A home teaching service was also seen as a useful way of maintaining good home–school communication. This service was monitored on a weekly basis by one of the Portage home teachers (Cameron, *op. cit.*).

At Heltwate School, Peterborough, the Portage home visiting scheme was introduced in 1978 after discussions between school staff and educational psychologists working locally (Hallmark and Dessent, 1982). The scheme arose because of the need to extend the school's work with selected pre-schoolers to children *other than those who were likely to be admitted to the school later* (Hallmark, 1983).

At Heltwate, a pilot Portage project scheme involving interested agencies and personnel was established relatively quickly for children who had a wide range of needs including 'mental handicap, moderate developmental delay and social-behavioural difficulties'. By 1982, the home teaching project had become an established permanent service with four members of the school staff visiting homes each week. The Peterborough Portage project was described as 'representing one way in which the school could extend services to other children with special needs, most of whom are unlikely to enter the school' (Hallmark and Dessent, *op. cit.*).

Although other school-based home teaching services do exist, a notable example being Forelands School, Broadstairs, they are relatively rare phenomena in the education world. Yet the need for such services has been highlighted by the recent report on *Educational Opportunities For All* (Fish, 1985). In particular, the Fish Report recommended that 'home visiting teaching arrangements to provide systematic early intervention programmes for parents and their children should be made more widely available within the authority'.

It is possible, therefore, that recommendations like this may encourage teachers to move out of their classrooms and into homes, particularly where there are families who have a handicapped pre-school child.

Portage as a school support model

One result of the 1981 Education Act has meant that an increasing number of pupils who have special educational needs are being catered for in mainstream settings. This is an important educational development but, as Jewell and Booth (1985) have noted, it has led to increasing concern from parents, teachers and support professionals about the kind of teaching which such children should receive.

One particularly ingenious way of providing practical support for teachers has been pioneered at Heltwate School (Rider and Keogh, 1982; Hallmark, *op. cit.*) where a 'mainstream support service' enables members of staff to visit primary and secondary schools where there are children with special needs, agree appropriate teaching targets with their class teachers, design a teaching strategy for attaining these teaching targets and return one week later to monitor the teaching outcome. The visiting Heltwate teachers meet weekly to discuss the work completed and any problems encountered. A supervisor, a senior member of the school staff, is responsible for coordinating the activities of all visiting teachers and making recommendations, some of which may have implications for the school, e.g. additional curriculum or resource requirements. In 1982, four members of Heltwate's 15 staff were working in five schools and providing a service for up to 100 pupils 'some of whom would have been transferred to a special school had it not been for this intervention' (Hallmark and Dessent, *op. cit.*).

A parallel remedial teaching support service has been taking shape at Weeke Infant School, Winchester, for the past two years (White, 1984a). Two teachers from the Winchester Portage home teaching service work closely with classroom teachers of a number of pupils who are experiencing difficulties with the mainstream curriculum. Having established a general background to the child's performance and completed an assessment of needs in the problem area, the visiting teacher introduces the first of a series of teaching activities using a school adapted version of the Portage activity chart (see Figure 1, p.63). Each activity is practised every day and the child's responses are recorded on the daily chart. Activities for the future are designed according to the success of the previous week and take the child through another small step in learning (White, *op. cit.*).

Both the above projects report considerable success in providing regular support for teachers in mainstream schools. Part of this success is ensured by the back-up provided by a positive monitoring component and continuity has been maintained by senior school management who have viewed such projects as central to school organization and not just as an appendage to the normal school day.

Portage and learning difficulties

In a series of papers (Booth and Jewell, 1983; Jewell and Booth, 1985; Miller *et al.*, 1985) a new project for the delivery of educational programmes for children with learning difficulties in mainstream schools was described. A programme for training teachers in the use of individual programmes and programme evaluation has been field tested and a management structure (closely mirroring the Portage home teaching model) has been recommended.

The pyramid monitoring model (see Figure 2, p.64) utilizes key school staff and also involves visiting support staff (and parents). The teaching technology involved represents an ingenious combination of direct instruction, precision teaching and Portage procedures. The most powerful components of these three models have been combined to produce a teaching formula for children who are experiencing difficulties in the basic subjects. This teaching is designed to allow such pupils to attain high levels of accuracy (see Figure 3, p.65) and fluency (see Figure 4, p.66).

The advantages of this support for mainstream teachers are obvious and include regular discussions on planning, teaching assessment and evaluation of curriculum objectives. In addition, the resource implications for local authorities become clearer and the monitoring pyramid ensures that the expertise of scarce supporting professionals is more effectively utilized.

A note of caution

Not all attempts to introduce Portage into schools have been a resounding success, however. Frederickson and Haran (1986) report that following a highly successful Portage workshop designed for staff in a day nursery, it was noted that a number of workshop participants reported no usage of activity charts over a six-month period. As a result, the authors have argued for 'flexibility and experimentation in supporting the integration and incorporation of the ideas presented during Portage training'.

The outcome of this study contrasts quite considerably with that reported by Miller *et al.* (*op. cit.*). Teachers generally valued the techniques of their workshop for children with special needs and 'persisted in their regular use over considerable periods of time'. One major difference between these two projects was that Miller and his colleagues set up a management structure which 'served to maintain the motivation of all concerned'.

Both directly and indirectly these studies demonstrate that

successful changes can only take place in organizations like schools where there is a management structure which encourages maintenance and continuation. Hard-pressed class teachers are unlikely to continue time and energy consuming activities unless they are specifically encouraged to do so and have a forum for discussing problems when these arise. Many of the guidelines set out in the NPA publication *A Guide to Setting up a Portage Service* are just as pertinent for the setting up and maintenance of school-based projects as they are for home-based schemes. Carefully planned services cannot afford to rely solely on endless enthusiasm or cumulative cooperation!

Some thoughts for the future

So far, the use of the Portage model in school has been mainly restricted to the primary and special education sectors. At a first glance, it may be less easy to see the relevance of what was originally a *pre-school* scheme to *secondary* education, but possibilities do exist. Within a school, it is not impossible to envisage a special needs coordinator using the Portage model as a school-support scheme for subject teachers who are likely to be faced with increasing numbers of pupils who have special educational needs. Outside school, an even more obvious area where aspects of the Portage model could be utilized is with the increasingly popular 'Paired' and 'Shared' reading schemes which have had remarkable success in involving parents in teaching basic subjects (especially reading) to pupils who have marked difficulties in these subject areas. (See Topping and Wolfendale (1985) for an account of school projects which involved parents in teaching reading skills.) In these home-based schemes, school-based coordinators might wish to avail themselves of the structured teaching technology, the detailed recording procedures and the positive monitoring component of the Portage model.

   On a final and more general note, the issue of 'integration' has dominated the educational world of the 1980s and has been the subject for both supportive and concerned debates. The *long-term* aim of an integrated system of education may be a powerful guiding concept in education, but it is less than clear where and how we should proceed at present. This uncertainty has been succinctly highlighted by Lindsay (1985) in his overview of a major conference which had as its theme, 'Integration: possibilities, practice and pitfalls'. He concluded:

> We must go beyond the rhetoric. The issue now is not *whether* to integrate children but *how* to integrate them to their advantage.

It has now become glaringly obvious that merely putting pupils with special educational needs in mainstream classrooms, and hoping that all will turn out for the best, is a likely recipe of failure for pupils and teachers alike. What the Portage model can offer to schools is a modest support system for both the teacher in school and the 'teachers' at home. Portage represents one strategy for operationalizing the fair-minded but fuzzy concept of 'integration'.

Figure 1: The activity chart adapted for use in Weeke Infant School (after White, 1984a)

Child's name	Number of chart
Visiting teacher's name	Date – first day of practice
Class teacher's name	Success rate – performance over one week

Teaching objective: the behaviour you want to see the child carrying out in one week's time

Directions for carrying out the teaching activity. These will include:

Materials: include each item, e.g. flashcards, books, number material, etc., that is to be used

Place of work: where and under what conditions the activity will be carried out, e.g. in the classroom or outside, sitting alone or with a group

Presentation: the way in which the materials are set out; the words that you use when carrying out the activity with the child; the number of prompts or cues that you give

Reinforcement: the way in which you show the child that he has made the correct response – this must be very clear to the child

Correction procedure: the help that you will give the child if he or she fails to make the correct response – this can be one of the following:

        you guide the child through the correct response

        you demonstrate the correct response and the child imitates you

        you correct the child verbally and he is able to make the correct response on second try

        you choose the minimum method of help to ensure that the child achieves the target

How to record: if the child carries out the activity according to the directions

        if the child carries out the activity with help as listed under correction procedure

Note: the child will always be successful either independently or with help

Objectives: each response the child makes during the activity						

DAYS

Figure 2:   A management structure for the delivery of educational programmes to children with learning difficulties in mainstream schools (after Miller *et al.*, 1985)

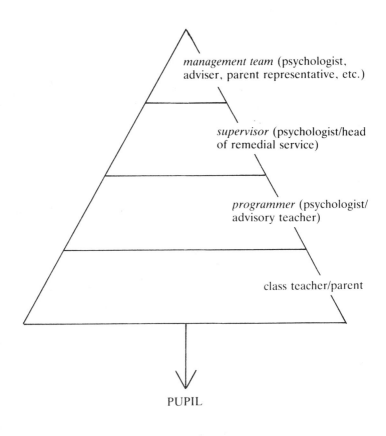

management team (psychologist, adviser, parent representative, etc.)

supervisor (psychologist/head of remedial service)

programmer (psychologist/ advisory teacher)

class teacher/parent

PUPIL

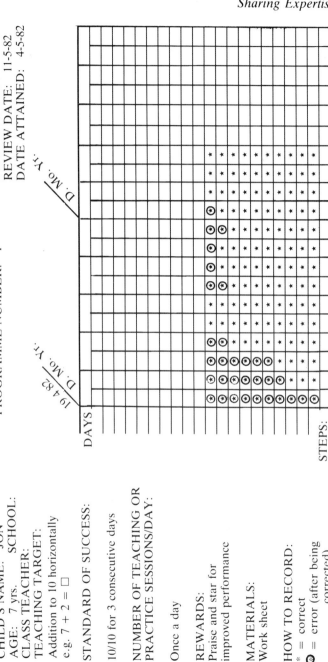

CHILD'S NAME: JON
AGE: 7 yrs.   SCHOOL:
CLASS TEACHER:
TEACHING TARGET:
Addition to 10 horizontally
e.g. $7 + 2 = \square$

PROGRAMME NUMBER: 1

DATE STARTED: 19-4-82
REVIEW DATE: 11-5-82
DATE ATTAINED: 4-5-82

STANDARD OF SUCCESS:

10/10 for 3 consecutive days

NUMBER OF TEACHING OR
PRACTICE SESSIONS/DAY:

Once a day

REWARDS:
Praise and star for
improved performance

MATERIALS:
Work sheet

HOW TO RECORD:
* = correct
⊙ = error (after being
    corrected)

Figure 3: Accuracy chart for teaching basic skills in a school setting (Booth and Jewell, 1983)

Figure 4:   A fluency chart for teaching basic skills in a school setting (Jewell and Booth, 1985)

Child's Name: Mark

Age: 7 years   School: —

Class Teacher/Parent: —

Teaching Objective:
   Says letter sounds (all alphabet)

Programme Number: 2

Date Started: 5.7.82

Review Date: 31.7.82

Date Attained:

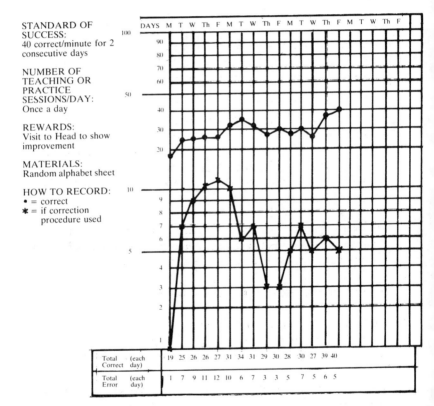

STANDARD OF SUCCESS:
40 correct/minute for 2 consecutive days

NUMBER OF TEACHING OR PRACTICE SESSIONS/DAY:
Once a day

REWARDS:
Visit to Head to show improvement

MATERIALS:
Random alphabet sheet

HOW TO RECORD:
• = correct
✱ = if correction
      procedure used

Total Correct (each day)	19	25	26	26	27	31	34	31	29	30	28	30	27	39	40
Total Error (each day)	1	7	9	11	12	10	6	7	3	3	5	7	5	6	5

CHAPTER 5
Using and Developing the Portage Teaching Materials

Mollie White

Mollie White is Lecturer in Pre-school Education at King Alfred's College of Education, Winchester, Hants., and Secretary of the National Portage Association. Since 1976 she has been a home teacher on the Winchester Portage Home Teaching Service.

The *Portage Guide to Early Education* represents one of the success stories of the last decade. The Guide was designed to support a home teaching intervention pioneered in Wisconsin by a team led by David and Marsha Shearer. Their aim was to introduce precision teaching techniques into the parents' daily care of the young child with special needs by:

> directly involving parents in the education of their children, by teaching parents what to teach, what to reinforce, and how to observe and record behaviour. (Shearer and Shearer, 1972)

The Portage teaching materials assist this process. They comprise:

> A *Checklist* composed of 580 behavioural items arranged in five major developmental areas covering birth to six years with an introductory section covering the first six months (Bluma *et al.*, 1976).
> A set of *Activity Cards*, one for each item on the checklist carrying suggestions for teaching the listed items.
> A *Portage Activity Chart* with instructions for use.

Each component of the teaching materials was designed to serve a specific function in the teaching process. This chapter examines the successes and weaknesses of the materials in use and considers ongoing and future developments designed to meet changing needs.

The system pioneered by the Shearers and their team focuses on a weekly visit to the home by a trained home visitor. During initial visits parents and home visitor together observe and record the child's existing progress and skills. A set of teaching activities is then designed based on these skills which aim to stimulate further development. Practice of the teaching activities is integrated into the parents' and the child's daily routines and a daily record is made of the child's progress. Precision teaching techniques are used to structure the design of the teaching activities: home visitors are trained in the use of these techniques and introduced to the Portage teaching materials which support their use during an initial three-day workshop (Shearer and Shearer, 1972).

Ongoing support is offered to the home visitor through a regular weekly meeting attended by fellow home visitors and a supervisor experienced in the use of precision teaching methods. Home visitors, who include volunteers and supervisors, come from a wide variety of professional and non-professional backgrounds. As members of a Portage team they aim to offer mutual support based on their multi-disciplinary backgrounds. Termly reports of the work carried out by the Portage team are prepared by the supervisor and presented to a management team from all the contributing disciplines and from parents. The success of the team's work with families is measured on positive changes in the child's behaviour resulting from the teaching programmes carried out by the parents.

The Portage materials act as teaching tools made available to the home visitors and families to assist in the design of the teaching programmes.

The Portage checklist

The checklist was designed by the original project staff in Wisconsin (Bluma *et al.*, 1976) as a curriculum guide to the planning of teaching programmes for individual children. The 580 behavioural items are presented in five developmental sequences covering the first six years of life headed *socialization, language, self-help, cognitive* and *motor* and preceded by an introductory section entitled *infant stimulation* which covers development during the first six months. The checklist serves two major functions: the establishment of a baseline of the child's skills on entry to the project and suggestions for appropriate teaching targets which build on those skills.

Success of the checklist

Initial response to the checklist by its major users, parents and home visitors, was enthusiastic. The presentation, which allowed ready access to the separate developmental areas, was attractive, both through its colour coding and the simple language generally used to describe each behavioural item. Parents, unfamiliar with such detailed descriptions of early development, found in the checklist a structure which enabled them to record their extensive knowledge of their child's behaviour. For many parents this was a very therapeutic exercise. Most of their previous experiences in relation to their child's development had been entirely focused on the child's deficits. The opportunity to examine in detail the skills which the child had already acquired despite the recognition of serious delay, was an opportunity to look positively at the child's progress so far (White, 1979).

Indeed many parents, so used to the emphasis on the child's slow development, found themselves surprised by the number of acquired skills revealed by the checklist.

Home visitors were also enthusiastic. Many had received little extended formal training in early child development and like the parents found the detail offered by the checklist to be very supportive during their initial examination of the child's entry skills. Moreover the positive parental response to this process offered a productive beginning to the crucial home visitor/parent relationship. Together, this 'home team' was able to assemble relatively quickly a detailed profile of the child's existing skills and the background to those skills.

The second purpose of the checklist, its use as a curriculum tool, was also well received by the parents. The structure which had enabled them to record their daily experience of their child's behaviour also offered ready access to teaching targets. Examination with the home visitor of missing items in the child's profile under each heading, discussion of recently acquired skills, and consideration of the following behavioural items in the

Age Level	Card	Behaviour	Entry Behaviour	Date Achieved	Comments
	28	Imitates movements of another child at play	✓	/ /	
1–2	29	Imitates adult in simple task (shakes clothes, pulls at bedding, holds silverware)		/ /	dusts! likes following me around
	30	Plays with one other child, each doing separate activity	✓	/ /	
	31	Takes part in game, pushing car or rolling ball with another child 2–5 minutes	?	/ /	only lasts a minute
	32	Accepts parents' absence by countinuing activities, may momentarily fuss	✓	/ /	
	33	Actively explores his environment	✓	/ /	
	34	Takes part in manipulative game (pulls string, turns handle) with another person	✓	/ /	
	35	Hugs and carries doll or soft toy		/ /	
	36	Repeats actions that produce laughter and attention	✓	/ /	Yes!
	37	Hands book to adult to read or share with him		/ /	
	38	Pulls at another person to show them some action or object		/ /	
	39	Withdraws hand, says "no-no" when near forbidden object with reminders		/ /	
	40	Waits for needs to be met when placed in high chair or on changing table		/ /	
	41	Plays with 2 or 3 peers		/ /	
	42	Shares object or food when requested with one other child		/ /	
	43	Greets peers and familiar adults when reminded		/ /	

Figure 1: Section of Portage checklist completed by a parent and a home teacher

sequence provided ample material for joint selection of future teaching objectives. (See Figure 1.)

The checklist acted as a vital tool in the process of negotiation between parent and Portage team which is a vital element in the Portage teaching model. It enabled a partnership to develop from the outset of the teaching.

Problems arising from the use of the checklist

While recognizing the attractions of the checklist for most parents and home visitors for what could be described as its 'user friendly' qualities, some professionals, highly trained in specific areas of early child development, expressed serious criticisms:

1 Behavioural items in the checklist are described in general terms and carry no clear criteria for attainment. Parents and home visitors can regard a behaviour as successfully attained which may not meet the standard required if items which follow are to be taught successfully.

2 Skills listed in the checklist under separate headings are taught as discrete items and the teaching model offers no guarantee that teaching will be initiated to generalize these skills into the child's spontaneous behaviour or linked to related skills in other areas of the checklist.

3 Behaviours in the Portage checklist were taken from psychometric tests by the Wisconsin team. Items present in such tests were measures of specific skills related to milestones of development in a 'normal' pre-school population. The checklist's reliance on these materials, rather than on data obtained from detailed observation of the many subskills covered in the learning process leading to the acquisition of major skills, has resulted in important omissions from the checklist sequences. Physiotherapists for example might argue that as a result of item Motor 16, 'Maintains sitting position for two minutes', a child can be 'placed' in a sitting position and the child's ability to maintain that position for a given number of seconds measured *before* important subskills such as the child's ability to bear weight through the arms is practised.

Despite the popularity of the checklist with parents and home visitors they too expressed problems:

4   Checklist items do not always succeed in pinpointing emerging behaviour leading to the selection of appropriate weekly teaching targets. This problem was identified most frequently with the multiply handicapped child and the very young child (Dessent and Ferguson, 1984; White and East, 1983).

5   Individual items within the checklist represent uneven steps in learning. For some items, the application of task analysis of major teaching techniques in the Portage teaching model does not provide a breakdown of subskills which relate to the child's existing level of development as revealed by the checklist. When professional expertise was sought to assist with these problems, additional teaching targets were identified which needed to be inserted earlier in the sequence (White and East, *op. cit.*).

6   The language used by the checklist has American connotations which are not always familiar to British users. In addition some items relate to an American culture and are not appropriate to families in the United Kingdom. This problem is exacerbated when families concerned come from cultural minorities (Bardsley and Perkins, 1985; Weihl, 1986).

7   Home visitors finding problems with particular areas of the checklist designed a smaller number of teaching activities for those areas. The focus on weekly success encouraged an avoidance of the more difficult curriculum areas (May and Schortinghuis, 1984).

The Portage activity cards

Appropriate use of the Portage activity cards can go a long way towards meeting some of these problems. They were designed to be used in conjunction with the checklist and when used alongside they offer important additional information to that provided by the checklist items. Each card carries a number of suggestions for teaching the listed item. If the child is able to carry out the listed skill according to *all* the suggestions on the card then a high level of attainment is assured.

The teaching suggestions themselves act as an important resource to families and to Portage workers whose experience of young children is limited. All the ideas presented on the cards have been used successfully within the home setting by the Wisconsin team and they represent a wealth of combined experience.

Problems arising from use of the cards

Unfortunately the emphasis in Portage training workshops on the need to respond to the individual's preferences when planning the teaching programmes has led to a misunderstanding of the role of the activity cards in programme planning. Focus on materials and rewards which relate to the child's experience, and concern given to the family environment and to family routines to produce teaching activities that are 'tailored' to each family's needs, distract attention from the activity cards. Workshop participants are encouraged to build on the child's emerging responses to her/his personal environment rather than impose activities derived from the activity card suggestions. Indeed the opportunity to teach through the child's individual responses is a major strength of the Portage teaching model and accounts for its success.

There is a danger however that parents and home visitors may neglect a *parallel variety* of teaching activities to those suggested by the cards. This danger is intensified when the child's rate of learning is slow and progress through a set of activities geared to one teaching concept is long drawn out.

In Figure 2, the not inconsiderable variety of activities represent a long process for *any* child acquiring early concepts of size, but it is a process vital to high quality learning. The importance of *maintaining* a programme over a specified time period is not made clear through the Portage materials.

The Portage activity chart

The Portage activity chart is without doubt the most important component of the Portage teaching materials. The instructions for writing a Portage activity chart (Figure 3) aim to ensure a response from home visitor and parent that will guarantee a successful small step in the child's behaviour *within one week*. Home visitors, after a

cognitive 32

AGE 2-3

TITLE: Points to big and little upon request

WHAT TO DO:

1. Collect big and little versions of the same type of objects, i.e. (big and little envelops, pencils, stones, shoes, coats, dishes, cookies, marshmallows, chairs, cars).
2. Place a big and little pencil in front of child. Ask him to make a mark on paper with the big pencil. Praise success. Repeat activity with other objects.
3. Ask child to find big and little objects around the house.
4. Have parent or teacher name big and little objects for the child for a week. After this have the child begin pointing to the big and little objects.
5. Do motor activities such as taking big steps, little steps, big jumps, little jumps, sit in a big chair, little chair.

Figure 2: A Portage teaching card

WINCHESTER PORTAGE
SERVICE ACTIVITY CHART

Child's Name:
Home Teacher's Name:
Week of:
CHECKLIST NUMBER:

Teaching Target
– write here the behaviour you want to
see from the child in one week's time.

Criterion
– the level of success you expect from
the child after one week's practice.

Recording
– write down the number of times you
want to record the behaviour you are
teaching on the *vertical* line of the graph.
– write the days of the week along the
horizontal line, beginning on the first
day of teaching.

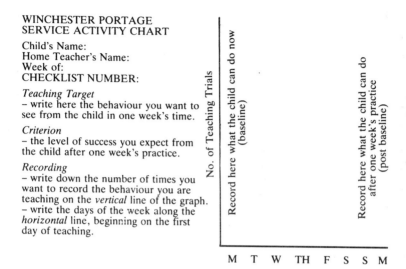

No. of Teaching Trials

Record here what the child can do now
(baseline)

Record here what the child can do
after one week's practice
(post baseline)

M   T   W   TH   F   S   S   M

Directions
Directions for practising the teaching activity should always explain what to do and
say when introducing the activity and also include the following information:-

Materials
– mention each item or toy that you use.

Place of Work
– make it clear where the activity should be carried out e.g. at the table, on the floor.

Presentation
– write down precisely what you will do and the words you will say to stimulate the
child to carry out the behaviour you are teaching.

Reinforcement for Success
– write down what you will do and say to show the child that he/she has attained the
target behaviour. This must be clearly different to your response when the child
needs help to attain the target.

Correction (or Teaching) Procedure
– write down the minimum help you will provide if the child needs help to attain the
target. This will be one of the following depending on the needs of the child:-
  a) you will give a verbal correction
  b) you will demonstrate to the child the correct behaviour
  c) you will guide the child physically through the correct behaviour
Always emphasize the *correct* behaviour.

Practice
– write down how many times the activity should be practised each day.

Recording
– record ✓ if the child attains the target behaviour according to the directions.
    ⊘ if the child needed help to attain the target behaviour according to the
    directions.

Figure 3:   The rules for writing an activity chart

relatively short period of training, are able to produce successful teaching activities following these directions. While there may be dispute about the effectiveness of the curriculum materials to generate and maintain appropriate teaching objectives, *the design model for the teaching exemplified in the chart is universally acclaimed.*

It is significant that while particular Portage services have made adaptations to the layout of the original chart demonstrated by the Wisconsin team these adaptations do not leave out any of the original components. Some objections to the terminology used by the Portage chart have produced variations in language: 'where', 'when' and 'how', for 'place of work', 'time of day' and 'presentation' in a chart used in a Liverpool nursery school project (Copley *et al.*, 1986) or the terms 'success procedure' for 'reinforcement' and 'teaching procedure' for 'correction procedure' in the Winchester service chart directions. Additional components have been added to charts: many teams include the 'long-term objective' and 'existing skill level', *but the structure for the teaching design remains the same.*

The success of the chart is owed to a number of factors:

1   The precision of the directions offers tight control of the teaching process.
2   The daily record of teaching trials provides ongoing data of the child's progress which can be shared with a wide number of people.
3   The analysis of the conditions embodied in the activity chart directions offers a set of variables that can be modified to fit a number of purposes:
    i   they can take into account the responses and the environment of each individual child and family;
    ii   they offer a number of options to enable supervisors, home visitors and parents to make changes to teaching activities which have failed;
    iii manipulation of these variables can bring about transfer and generalization of acquired skills;
    iv   the expertise of associated professionals can be made available to the non-specialist by a process of observation of the professional at work according to the activity chart components (Figure 4);

WINCHESTER PORTAGE SERVICE
ACTIVITY CHART

Child's Name: Lesley
Home Teacher's Name:
Week Of:
Checklist No.:

Teaching Target: Lesley will sit on Mother's knee without extension for periods of one minute		HT	M		HT	M
	3					
	2					
Criterion: one out of three trials	1					

Days

Directions: (Please check that you have included: materials [✓] place of
work [✓] presentation [✓] reinforcement [✓] correction
procedure [✓] and how often to practice [✓].)

Sit on a chair with Lesley on your knee. Have him with his back towards your
front with a gap between you. Put his legs either side of your legs.
Place your hands on his shoulders with the palms of your hands on his
shoulder blades.
Rock him *very gently* backwards and forwards. Sing or talk to Lesley as you
do this.
If he remains relaxed for the one minute period give him a cuddle and praise
him.
If he begins an extension during the one minute period, use the pressure of
your hands to bring his shoulders into a forward position and lean him
forward from his hips. Keep him in this position until he is again relaxed.
Continue with the rocking game for a further minute.

Method of Recording:
✓ Lesley sits on your knee without extension for one minute
Ⓐ Lesley needs your help to avoid an extension

This chart is included in Smith *et al.* (1977)

Figure 4:   Illustrating the use of activity chart instructions to process
information provided by an associated professional (here a
physiotherapist)

v   the charts act as a direct communication concerning the teaching between parents, home visitor, Portage team and management team members.

Problems

Producing a well-designed teaching activity can be a lengthy operation and fulfilling all the conditions imposed by the chart a demanding exercise. Activity charts in practice do not always include all the information required by the directions. Nevertheless it is the structure provided by the chart that enables home visitors and parents to teach the child effectively. Failed activities can only be analysed when *all* the information is available to the support team.

The activity chart is appropriate to small-step learning. It is designed to meet the needs of children whose development shows delay equal to one year in a specific area of development. Parents helping children whose rate of learning exceeds the need to practise a specific structured activity each day for one week may require only the identification of a teaching objective supported by a variety of materials and presentations over a small space of time in order to meet the required goal. The activity chart variables can be used in this situation to structure daily changes in presentation.

Additional aspects of Portage

Tony Dessent's final address at the Cambridge Portage Conference in 1982 expressed a concern shared by many home visitors and families that the activity chart data represented only one part of the activities carried out alongside the teaching model. For some parents, these additional activities were more important than the teaching activities. Advice and information on support groups, playgroups, local services, grants and equipment and educational information were sought by families (Dessent, 1984). For some families the opportunity to talk to the home visitor about their feelings towards their child and about their role as parents was very important. Le Poidevin and Cameron (1985) discussed the relationship between parent and home visitor outside the teaching situation. The failure of the Portage teaching model either to record or offer direct support in relation to these activities was considered a major problem by many people using it.

Recent developments in Portage practice

Many of the criticisms outlined above have been resolved since the introduction of the Portage teaching model into the UK and its evaluation by the Wessex Health Care Evaluation Research Team led by Dr Albert Kushlick (Smith *et al.*, 1977). Adaptations have been made to the model itself and new materials have been designed in response to specific needs. The earliest of these adaptations was the concept of long-term goal setting.

Long-term goal setting

Initial Portage workshops now recommend regular long-term goal setting in relation to each individual child. Parents, home visitors, supervisor and Portage team members, plus associated professionals concerned with the child, jointly identify acquired skills; select new objectives; discuss the best means to meet these objectives and assemble and circulate this information to everyone concerned with the teaching and care of the child.

The sharing of a wide range of expertise during the goal setting exercise meets many of the criticisms levelled at the Portage teaching model concerning the choice of inappropriate objectives in response to the checklist and the failure to teach important subskills.

Generalization and adaptation of acquired skills

A paper at the Cambridge Conference (Cameron, 1984b) highlighted the problem of generalization and adaptation. This speaker offered a model originally developed by Haring and colleagues (1978) which enables skills acquired through structured teaching to be taught to 'fluency', 'generalization' and 'adaptation' levels. No changes however were proposed to the Porfage teaching procedures which could guarantee the implementation of teaching procedures involved in Haring's model. Two years later at the Liverpool Conference a proposal was made (White, 1986) that specific additions should be made both to the weekly home visit and to the long-term goal planning exercise:

(a)   long-term goal planning to include specific play suggestions aimed at recently acquired skills;

(b)   a regular play session to be built into the weekly home visit for the practice of these skills;

(c)   the inclusion of regular activity charts aimed at the transfer of newly acquired skills.

The objective behind these proposals was to set up *play conditions* within the home relevant to the child's skills which because of their self-reinforcing nature would increase fluency and ultimate generalization and adaptation.

The original Portage materials offer support for this exercise. The activity cards provide a wide variety of suggestions for maintenance purposes including many play presentations. The components of the Portage activity chart (Figure 3) offer an analysis of conditions which can be modified to create small-step changes in the design of appropriate play opportunities. Such an approach to task analysis can be shared by members of the Portage team during the long-term planning process.

Finally, suggestions circulated at the Third Annual Portage Conference in Liverpool (White, 1986) to support these proposals directed Portage teams and families towards pre-school settings and pre-school literature outside the Portage teaching model. Observing the play of 'normal' children when practising specific skills offers a rich source of additional ideas for planned play sessions.

A checklist for the multiply handicapped child

The checklist was designed by the authors in response to problems they encountered during their work with the Peterborough Portage team (Dessent and Ferguson, 1984). They found the selection of teaching objectives, capable of showing measurable change within one week, a continuing difficulty when designing programmes for multiply handicapped children. What was needed was a checklist of skills which was sensitive to very small components of behaviour in order to find starting points for the teaching. Their failure to find appropriate starting points through the Portage checklist led them to obtain help from associated professionals such as the physiotherapist and the occupational therapist.

Other developmental schedules designed for professionals working with multiply handicapped populations were also consulted and the objectives which resulted from these investigations presented in six core areas: 'feeding, communication, gross motor, auditory and visual skills, and socialization'. The format resembles the Portage checklist and includes 245 separate developmental items.

The success of the Dessent/Ferguson checklist highlights the need for support materials to meet the needs of specific populations. Other such materials have been reported by Portage practitioners, e.g. a checklist designed for the visually handicapped (Courtney, 1985). Making such materials available to a wider number of Portage teams is a task receiving attention from the National Portage Association.

The Wessex Revised Portage Language Checklist

NFER-Nelson have published a revision to the language section of the Portage checklist designed in response to problems encountered by Portage teams in Wessex and to meet criticisms of language teaching through the Portage teaching model (White and Ease, 1983; White, 1984b; and White and East, 1986).

The revised checklist has four major components: an expanded sequence; grouped behaviours; activity cards; and adult behaviours arranged in four separate year levels each of which features all four components.

1 The expanded sequence incorporates language behaviours from all areas of the checklist and adds new behaviours to provide a profile of development sensitive enough to generate appropriate small-step language objectives.

2   The Index of Grouped Behaviours responds to a different problem from that identified by White and East and Dessent and Ferguson (*op. cit.*) responding to weekly teaching objectives. It is the need to focus attention on the variety of *major skills* important to early language development. The authors intend that the identification of major skill areas such as 'listening and attending' will prompt home visitors and parents to aim for high quality skills in each major skill area.

3   The activity cards provide teaching suggestions appropriate to sustained practice of each acquired skill; many of these relate to play settings.

4   Finally, the adult behaviours in each section alert home visitor and parent to monitor their own language behaviour in relation to the individual child. The authors recommend that where necessary, activities should be designed to bring about changes in *adult* behaviour in order to set up appropriate conditions for effective communication between adult and child. (See White and East, *op. cit.*, for a discussion of this point.)

The adult behaviours are also useful to home visitors and parents when they consider the 'presentation' of tasks in other areas of the checklist. Examples of these two uses of the adult behaviours are given in the revised checklist.

Future developments

Response to the additional components of the revised checklist has been positive and plans for similar revisions to the remaining checklist areas are in motion supported by the National Portage Association and NFER-Nelson. The usefulness in future revisions of presenting behaviours in a continuous sequence and also in major skill areas has been questioned. Processing the information provided by the sequence to highlight areas of strength and weakness and indicate related skills has been a longstanding need. Gardner and Judson (1982) presented a curriculum model at the First Portage Conference. This provided a structure for relating checklist behaviours into component groups of increasing difficulty to assist long-term goal planning. There is an argument in the face of reported consumer satisfaction with such groupings for presenting the entire checklist according to such arrangements and abandoning the traditional sequence. Discussion with parents new to the Portage teaching model however reveals a marked preference for an 'initial' response to the sequenced arrangement; it matches their 'general' observation of their child. In addition the recording of a *continuing* number of items present in the child's repertoire under each area heading is reinforcing during the early assessment period. Interpreting the information for teaching purposes is more appropriate at a later stage.

The role of the National Portage Association

Adaptations to the Portage teaching model and revised versions of the teaching materials have occurred as a direct response by Portage users to the needs of the families they serve. The annual Portage Conference has provided practitioners with a valuable opportunity to share their experiences and to exchange reports on current practice; the publication of the proceedings of these conferences by NFER-Nelson has been a major contribution to the successful dissemination of ongoing developments. There is however a continuing need for information relating to Portage practice and materials that cannot be met solely through the published materials.

Information on practice which responds to specific needs, e.g. cultural minorities and special populations, is in great demand. The identification of such practice has become a major concern of the National Portage Association. The establishment of regional study days and the development of the Advanced Portage Workshop are opportunities for the Association to make available materials which promote good practice both in relation to the teaching model and to activities associated with it.

Future plans

In addition to their role in producing and circulating workshop and study materials, the National Portage Association is collaborating with NFER-Nelson to produce an updated British version of the Wisconsin *Guide to Early Education*. The new checklist will be published in the format described earlier; additional cards will be made available; UK equivalents produced for American terms and for behaviours specific to the United States; and a British manual produced to support the new materials.

The resource for this enterprise comes not only from the combined experience of National Portage Association members but also from those who work alongside Portage teams as associated professionals. The Association's role in bringing together the experience of the 'expert', the Portage team and the family is crucial. The integration of their widely ranging experience is an exciting prospect and one that is made possible by the structure offered by the Portage teaching model.

Conclusion

Criticisms of the materials which support the teaching model have resulted in useful modifications and adaptations both to the model and to the original materials. New materials have been disseminated and materials at the planning stage aim to support high quality teaching. The introduction of long-term goal setting to involve the collaboration of associated professionals and more recent developments which focus on planning activities directed at the maintenance, generalization and adaptation of recently acquired skills meet many of the criticisms of Portage teaching. Opportunities for parents and Portage teams to increase their skills in these areas is a major objective of the National Portage Association and a focus for the design of additional teaching materials.

Finally, materials which meet the growing demand for a formal response to activities taking place alongside the teaching model are emerging from parental participation in Portage workshops, conferences and study days. Dissemination of these materials on a wider scale is vital to further growth and development in the coming decade.

CHAPTER 6
Research and Evaluation: How Effective is Portage?

Robert J. Cameron

There can be few approaches on the UK educational scene which have spread with the rapidity of the Portage home teaching model. From its modest beginnings in 1976 as a pilot research project the scheme has spread throughout the British Isles to an extent that Bendall *et al.* (1984) in their National Survey were able to locate over 100 home teaching and almost 50 school- and centre-based schemes using the Portage model. This number is likely to increase by some 20 per cent as a result of the recently awarded Department of Education and Science educational support grant which has been made available for setting up new Portage home teaching schemes.

It seems clear therefore that Portage was not only the type of service which parents of pre-school children with special needs sought, but the approach had advantages which were obvious to the many supporting professionals from all disciplines (and volunteers) who set up and maintained Portage schemes all over the country. In retrospect, it would seem that Portage was one of those educational innovations which not only appeared at exactly the right time (the decade when parents were being 'rediscovered' as the major educators of their children in the early years) but which also fitted exactly into the 'services needed' jigsaw.

Home-based programmes

Today, it is blatantly obvious to anyone setting up an early intervention programme that home visiting services have considerable potential for enhancing the development of children

with special needs and their families. Such programmes can begin
before family problems become intractable, involve the people who
spend most of the time in direct contact with the child, and are
designed to be flexible enough to adjust to the often highly
idiosyncratic needs and strengths of individual families. It is
scarcely surprising therefore that in his recent historical review of
'effective teaching', Thomas (1985) concluded that: 'Given a few
early broadly defined parameters within which any reasonably
sensitive adult works with an individual child (e.g. enthusiasm,
patience, the ability and willingness to give encouragement) such
help can hardly fail to be successful'.

Evidence for the effectiveness of home-based interventions
comes from many different sources. Two of the most important are:

(a)   Comparisons of different parenting styles. Honig (1980)
summarized the difference between parents of both more able and
less able three-year-olds. Although many similarities were noted,
consistent parenting differences emerged. Chief among these were:
parents of more competent children modelled behaviours that they
wanted their children to perform rather than merely using words,
observed their child's performance and adjusted activities
accordingly, and set clear rules for behaviour and gave reasons for
these rules. In addition, the more 'successful' parents joined with
their children in the activities and allowed them to experiment with
materials around the house. In short, such parents *intuitively* used
many of the well-established basic techniques in good teaching.

(b)   Early intervention programmes. The parent involvement
element in the early intervention equation has been highlighted by
numerous researchers. Pointing to the successes of parent- or
family-centred early intervention programmes for handicapped
children, Tjossem (1976) argued that 'supportive services should be
initiated early, should be family orientated, should support and
enhance the mother/child interaction and should be sustained'.
Similarly, Bronfenbrenner (1974) in his survey of the effects of the
American Headstart Research Programme concluded: 'the
evidence indicates that the family is the most effective system of
fostering and sustaining the development of the child'. Without
family involvement 'any effects of intervention, at least in the
cognitive sphere, appeared to erode rapidly once the programme
ends' (Bronfenbrenner, *op. cit.*). In a later UK review, Cave and
Maddison (1978) also noted that the most successful early

intervention projects were those which 'involved parents and used a structured approach'.

Given the strength of this evidence, it is scarcely surprising that Lillie (1981) argued that the family was of prime importance and that the conventional notion of *separating a child from the home* and boosting his or her level of functioning through the application of professional expertise without reference to parents or home environment, should be rejected.

One of the most comprehensive surveys of the early intervention field has been carried out by Bricker *et al.* (1984). Bricker and her colleagues produced one of those delightfully acid academic reviews which dissolves almost every piece of research carried out during the past decade and leaves the reader with the empty feeling that very little in the field of early childhood intervention actually works (and even those few projects which show some promise only work inefficiently!). Despite their general gloom and doom, however, the reviewers grudgingly conclude 'early intervention programmes were generally supportive and helpful to parents of biologically developed infants'.

Evaluating Portage

While the rapid take-up of the Portage approach as a service for families who have a handicapped pre-schooler is prima facie evidence for its usefulness, it is of course necessary to consider more objective and 'harder' data. A considerable body of research findings on Portage has grown up over the past decade. Such studies have looked at a variety of different aspects of this home teaching model and asked questions about its effectiveness as a *home teaching service* for pre-school handicapped children, as a *support service* for parents, as a *general model* for early intervention and as an *educational approach* for future research and development.

A summary of the major research studies carried out both in the United States and the United Kingdom appears in the two Appendices to this chapter. The bulk of this research can be viewed as falling into four identifiable phases in the development of the Portage model over the past two decades. These are:

1   Implementation. Will it work?

This represents the earliest research phase and the questions which
were asked were: *can the Portage home teaching model enhance the
development of pre-school handicapped children* and *how does it
compare with other schemes which have similar objectives?* A
considerable amount of work in the early 1970s in the US and at a
later stage in the UK attempted to answer these two questions.

A summary of the early US evaluations appears in Cochrane and
Shearer (1984) and reported outcomes suggest that children who
received a Portage home teaching service had unexpectedly
accelerated development in terms of IQ, self-help skills, and
physical, social, language and academic development. These
studies also highlight the success of parents as teachers since an
average of 91 per cent of the activities taught by parents were
successfully attained by their children (Shearer and Shearer, 1972).

Other US studies in the implementation phase showed that both
trained and untrained professionals could deliver a Portage service
(Schortinghuis and Frohman, 1974) and indicated that the Portage
home teaching model could outperform a more traditional special
school programme (Peniston, 1972).

Although these results were convincing enough to persuade the
Joint Dissemination and Review Panel of the United States Office
of Education to validate the Portage project in 1975 as 'a model for
dissemination and replication throughout the country' (Cochrane
and Shearer, *op. cit.*) some educational sceptics might have been
more easily convinced of the effectiveness of a Portage service if
control group data had been presented. In the United Kingdom,
Revill and Blunden (1979a) attempted to remedy this possible
deficit by using a multi-baseline research design (where each child
acted as his or her own control). Reported outcomes of this study
(and an earlier piece of action research carried out by Smith *et al.*,
1977) showed that the children on the scheme made considerable
progress and the rate of progress was faster with Portage. Both
studies demonstrated that parental cooperation and satisfaction
was high.

2   Replication. Will it work elsewhere?

The next phase of Portage research was the replication phase and as the studies detailed in Appendices I and II show, the robustness and clarity of the Portage approach has demonstrated that its range of applicability extends well beyond Portage in Wisconsin. Between 1972 and 1974 nine replications of the Portage model were set up across the United States (Shearer and Loftin, 1984). Results showed that gains made by children at all the sites were similar to those made by children in the original Portage study (Shearer and Shearer, *op. cit.*). By 1977, the Portage scheme had been replicated in almost 60 other places in the United States and among cultures which varied from Eskimos to Navaho Indians to poor (and not so poor!) whites.

In the UK, work in the replication phase attempted to answer the question: 'can the Portage service be maintained after the initial enthusiasm has passed and after the research team support has been withdrawn?' A three-year follow-up of the original Portage research project in Winchester which had meantime become a local and health authority service (Castillo *et al.*, 1980) and a Welsh replication of the South Glamorgan project in neighbouring Dyfed (Revill and Blunden, 1979b) showed that child gains and parental satisfaction remained high.

3   Dissemination. Can others make it work?

In this phase, an answer was sought to the question: *can the scheme be disseminated to other areas, especially those with differing social and cultural features?* Shearer and Loftin (*op. cit.*) have recorded that work is now going on with 75 different nations and Portage schemes now exist in Africa, Australasia, Europe, North and South America and Asia. In addition, Portage teaching materials have now been translated into more than 11 languages (Shearer and Loftin, *op. cit.*) and Cantonese, Hindi and Gudgerati versions are in translation.

A particularly interesting dissemination programme in Peru has been reported (Jesien *et al.*, 1979; Jesien, 1983). As a result of this work, the Peruvian government has decided to use the Portage model as a basis for their new pre-school intervention programme.

As already mentioned, the spread of Portage within the United Kingdom has been rapid and the results of the first National Portage Survey (Bendall *et al.*, 1984; Bendall, 1985) provided fascinating data on the development and maintenance of 117 UK Portage home teaching schemes. A particularly thorough evaluation of the Portage home teaching model in South Lakeland, Cumbria, is reported by Myatt (1983) and numerous small-scale and unpublished Portage evaluations have been carried out throughout the British Isles.

In this section it is particularly gratifying to note the success of the Portage home teaching model in both first, second and third world settings. It is an impressive performance for a scheme which relies mainly on parents, uses supporting professionals sparingly and utilizes no complex educational technology or materials. Indeed, it is possible that the *simplicity* of the Portage approach has been one of its major assets and ensured its success internationally.

4   Adaptation. How can it be improved?

In many ways, the question '*how can the Portage model be improved?*' is a particularly exciting one and it is interesting to note parallels between the United States and the United Kingdom in some of the recommended adaptations and extensions of the original Portage home teaching model. Four additional components have been suggested by this ongoing research.

(a)   Helping families to deal with *family (non-educational) problems* (Shearer and Loftin, *op. cit.*; Cameron, 1985a; Land, 1985).

(b)   Ensuring that Portage children can *generalize and adapt* the skills which they have been taught (Shearer and Loftin, *op. cit.*; Cameron, 1984b).

(c)   Teaching *multiply handicapped* children (Barna *et al.*, 1980; Bidder *et al.*, 1982; Felce *et al.*, 1984; Kushlick *et al.*, 1985).

(d)   Teaching *early language* skills (Clements *et al.*, 1981; Vicary, 1985).

These likely directions for future research within the Portage model are discussed in Chapter 7. Since a considerable amount of work remains in all four areas, the adaptation phase is likely to be the longest stage in the life history of Portage: indeed, in the true spirit of evaluation, this phase will never be completed!

Some comments

If we attempt an overview of the work which is being carried out within Portage, we are likely to end up with something of a paradox. In the first place it is clear from the evidence summarized in both Appendices I and II that an impressive amount of basic research and service evaluation has already been carried out within the existing Portage model. Indeed, Frederickson and Haran (1986) argue it is now time for Portage evaluation studies to shift their focus from proving the effectiveness of the educational technology to 'an extended analysis of the important aspects of the approach in promoting children's learning in ways which are maximally compatible with the wider objectives, needs and pre-existing skills of direct contact personnel and each of the variety of settings in which the Portage model is currently being applied'.

Sturmey (1986) in a presentation to the Fifth National Portage Conference in Huddersfield identified a number of areas for 'extended analysis'. Chief among these was a suggestion that parents who were given training in *general principles* of behaviour modification might be able to tackle a wider range of different tasks for their child, *without the need for home teachers to model every task*. Similarly, Whittaker (1985) in a useful paper considers some of the possible limiting factors which might have to be taken into account when asking parents to work systematically with their children. All of these represent important variables which the Portage home teaching model cannot ignore: none appears to be insoluble!

Although the bulk of future Portage evaluation is likely to take place at the dissemination and adaptation levels, the other side of the paradox has to be considered. The need for further research at the implementation level, particularly to improve the specificity of reported results, remains as important now as it was in the early stages of development. We are forcibly reminded of this by Bricker *et al.* (*op. cit.*) who bemoan the fact that research analysis (at the implementation level) is described only in 'the most global fashion'. These researchers conclude: 'given the appeal and broad dissemination of this project [Portage], it is unfortunate that more specific information on the programme evaluations are lacking.'

It therefore appears that the apparently simple question 'does Portage work?' turns out to be suspiciously like that other simple question 'how long is a piece of string?' General questions of this type tend to conceal clusters of smaller and more specific queries. Questions about the effectiveness of home visiting schemes like Portage, as Gray and Wanderson (1980) point out, need to be rephrased as: 'what characteristics of home-based interventions are more effective in facilitating which areas of confidence?'

It is simply not possible to design the perfect evaluation that will definitively answer all these questions. What does seem clear however is, given the dearth of research evidence which usually accompanies the introduction of educational innovations, Portage, as Lister (1985) reminds us, is one of the *more carefully researched* educational approaches in use today. It is also highly gratifying to observe how the evaluative component of the Portage model has generated much research of both an initial and ongoing variety. Portage has supported the far from common research stance that there is no shame in not knowing, only in not wanting to know!

Appendix I: Portage home teaching model: US research

Research phase	Questions asked	Date of study	Source of published data	Numbers and research design	Reported outcome of study
Implementation phase	Does the Portage home teaching service enhance the development of pre-school children with special needs?	1970–71	Cochrane and Shearer (1984)	57 families: service evaluation	Children gained 18.3 IQ points over a 9-month period.
		1971–72	Shearer and Shearer (1972)	75 families: service evaluation	Average child gained 13 months developmentally over 8-month period. Also 91% of activities taught by parents successfully attained by children.
		1973–74	Cochrane and Shearer (1984)	130 families: service evaluation	Children had higher than predicted gains in self-help, physical, social communication and academic development.
	Does professional background effect home teaching?	1973–74	Schortinghuis and Frohman (1974)	16 families visited by professionals: 21 by para-professionals	Gains made by children served by trained and untrained professionals were similar.
	How does Portage home teaching compare with a school programme?	1971–72	Peniston (1972)	36 families in experimental group: 27 families in control group	Portage children made greater gains in mental age, IQ, language, academic development and socialization than children receiving a special school programme.

Research phase	Questions asked	Date of study	Source of published data	Numbers and research design	Reported outcome of study
Replication phase	Will the Portage model work with different disorders and in different social contexts?	1972–74	Portage Project Report to Joint Dissemination Panel of USOE, 1975 (Also reported in Shearer and Loftin, 1984)	Families from 9 replication sites: inter-group comparison	Gains made by children at all sites were similar to those made by children in the original Portage study (Shearer and Shearer, 1972).
Dissemination phase	Can the Portage approach be used effectively outside the US context?	1975	Shearer and Loftin (1984)	Work with 75+ nations: replication evaluation	Portage schemes now exist in Africa, Australia, Europe, N and S America and Asia. Portage materials have been translated into 11 languages.
	Can the Portage model be used as a pre-school intervention programme in a developing country?	1979–81	Jesien *et al.* (1979) Jesien (1983)	Urban: 120 exptal and 115 control Rural: 60 exptal and 40 control families	Children on urban programme gained on general cognitive and perceptual motor abilities. Children on rural programme gained on general cognitive and verbal abilities.
Adaptation phase	Can parents' teaching and management skills be improved?	1974–78	Boyd (1977) Also reported in Shearer and Loftin (1984)	48 families: inter-group comparison	Both the regular Portage model and the Portage Parent Programme were effective.

Research phase	Questions asked	Date of study	Source of published data	Numbers and research design	Reported outcome of study
Adaptation phase cont'd	Can the home teaching process be improved by modifications?	1975	Shearer and Loftin (1984)	Ongoing research project. No published evaluation data yet available	Suggested additions to the Portage model: 1 Informal child-centred activities to encourage skill generalization and to enhance parental independence in teaching. 2 Resource materials and information about other services provided for parents. 3 Opportunities to discuss family concerns and anxieties.

Appendix II: Portage home teaching model: UK research

Research phase	Questions asked	Date of study	Source of published data	Numbers and research design	Reported outcome of study
Implementation phase	Can the Portage model be operated in the UK context and using existing services?	May–Dec 1976	Smith *et al.* (1977)	13 families: pilot project evaluation	Child gains: 82% teaching objectives attained. Parent cooperation and satisfaction high.
		July–March 1977	Revill and Blunden (1979a)	19 families: multi-baseline design	Child gains: 88% of teaching objectives attained. Rate of skill acquisition faster with Portage. More skills learned other than those directly taught.
Replication phase	Can the Portage service be maintained after initial enthusiasm phase has passed and after research support has been withdrawn?	Oct–Dec 1979	Castillo *et al.* (1980) Revill and Blunden (1979b)	17 families: follow-up evaluation 6 families: in replication study	Child gains: 92% of teaching objectives attained. Parent cooperation and satisfaction remained high.

Research phase	Questions asked	Date of study	Source of published data	Numbers and research design	Reported outcome of study
Generalization phase	Can the Portage Model operate successfully in other UK contexts?	1982–83	Bendall *et al.* (1984) Bendall (1985)	117 Portage Schemes in UK: postal survey and in situ interviews	Results of first National Portage Survey of the extent of Portage type services in the UK were discussed.
		1980–83	Myatt (1983)	34 families in South Cumbria: contextual evaluation	Improved child progress and parental esteem.
Adaptation phase	What effect does a Portage service have on non-educational problems faced by families?	1977–78	Sandow and Clarke (1978)	32 families: experimental and control group comparison	Families who receive frequent visits from home teachers may become more dependent than less frequently visited families.
		1981–82	Holland and Noaks (1982)	14 families: service evaluation	Reduction in maternal depression follows Portage intervention.

Research phase	Questions asked	Date of study	Source of published data	Numbers and research design	Reported outcome of study
Adaptation phase cont'd		July 1978–July 1983	Cameron (1985a)	113 families: longitudinal evaluation	Low rates of divorce, parental depression and children received into care for Portage families.
		1983–84	Sampson (1984)	13 Portage parents, 17 parents not receiving Portage and 17 parents of non-handicapped children	Attitudes of Portage parents resembled the parents with normal children, i.e. they were more accepting of their children, and more positive about themselves as parents than other groups of parents of handicapped children.
		1984	Land (1985)	15 families: follow-up interviews	Portage service was valued by parents both in terms of help in promotion of their child's development and the help and support it provided to them as parents.
	Does the Portage model operate successfully for different degrees of disability?	1977–79	Barna *et al.* (1980)	35 families: within-group comparison	Environmentally deprived and developmentally delayed children progressed well. Cerebral palsy and visually handicapped children developed at a very slow rate.

Research phase	Questions asked	Date of study	Source of published data	Numbers and research design	Reported outcome of study
Adaptation phase cont'd		3-month period during 1982	Bidder *et al.* (1982)	38 families: within group comparison	Severely delayed and older Down's syndrome children made fewest gains on the checklist.
		3-month period during 1983	Felce *et al.* (1984)	24 severely and profoundly handicapped adults in residential care	Little evidence of skill acquisition was found.
	Does direct instruction help or hinder generalization and adaptation of learned skills?	1980–81	McConkey (1981)	Unknown number of participants: observational study	Direct instruction may not help children to generalize skills to new tasks.

Research phase	Question asked	Date of study	Source of published data	Numbers and research design	Reported outcome of study
Adaptation phase cont'd		1967–81 (US study)	Becker *et al.* (1981)	5050 follow through children and 3584 control group children	Direct instruction pupils performed best of all approaches in both basic skills and cognitive conceptual skills.
	Is the Portage model the most appropriate method for teaching language skills to pre-school children with special educational needs?	1980–81	Clements *et al.* (1981)	15 pre-school and school age children: experimental and control group comparison	No difference in the progress of (a) a pre-school group on a new language programme (b) the progress of a school age group (c) a Portage service group.
		1983–84	Vicary (1985)	12 mothers and their handicapped children. (6 families receiving a Portage service, 6 were not)	Portage parents vocalized more often and used more directive speech to their children.

CHAPTER 7
Developing the Portage Model: Some Directions for Applied Research*

Robert J. Cameron

Of all the changes which have occurred in the field of both mental and physical handicap over the past decade or so, one of the most significant has been the movement away from the old 'medical model' of handicap to the more recent 'psycho-educational approach'. Applying psychology, especially the powerful tools of behavioural psychology, has enabled parents, teachers and others involved with handicapped people to move away from a passive *caring* involvement to an active *teaching* role. The result has been that many handicapped people have acquired useful life skills which enable them to do things for and by themselves which, even ten years ago, might have elicited comments like 'They could never learn skills like these because they are just too handicapped'.

As well as affecting the work of direct contact people like parents, teachers, care staff, and nurses, these changes are reflected in the service delivery of the supporting professionals (for example, psychologists, social workers, psychiatrists). In retrospect, it does seem as though the 'bad old '50s and '60s' represented a period when both established and emerging professional groups erected barriers around their professional skills. Thus, doctors declared themselves as the custodians of mental handicap diagnosis and service allocation, teachers and nurses believed that they had a monopoly on teaching and nursing skills, and social agency workers saw themselves single-handedly supporting families with a handicapped member.

* This chapter is an abridged version of a paper which will appear in HEDDERLY, R. and JENNINGS, K. (Eds) (1986). *Extending and Developing Portage*. Windsor: NFER-NELSON (in press).

Hoarding professional skills may possibly increase the prestige and status of professional groups. In mental handicap, however, restrictive practices probably contributed to slow service development for the clients. Carefully guarded skills also encouraged the growth of a narrow, and often incestuous, field of knowledge. It also supported an 'illness model' rather than an 'educational model' of mental handicap. Most of all it acted as a barrier to sharing useful skills in applied psychology with other professional groups, especially direct contact professionals and parents.

Of all the changes which have taken place in the past two decades, the movement away *from hoarding to selling (or giving away) professional skills* is one which has been growing for some time and which continues to gather impetus.

Evaluation

Possibly no service takes the task of giving away skills so seriously as the Portage home teaching model, where the emphasis has always been on teaching parents of pre-schoolers with special needs to teach their own children (see Cochrane and Shearer (1984) for a summary of progress). This parents-as-teachers approach appears to have been remarkably successful and research evaluations of Portage services have indicated encouraging outcomes for children who have special needs and overwhelmingly positive consumer responses from their parents. A review of this evidence appears in Chapter 6 and if we add the several dozen unpublished pilot and research studies carried out at a local level, it is difficult to disagree with the comment made by Lister (1985): 'there are few other examples of a system which has been so thoroughly evaluated and which has been so enthusiastically received by parents'.

Developing Portage

Successful ventures eventually attract critical comments. In the case of Portage, this has tended to be general criticism of the kind which could be applied to most pre-school intervention programmes. Many of these general comments have been challenged by Cameron *et al.* (1984) who conclude that Portage 'stands up remarkably well as a service delivery model for parents who have a preschool child with special needs'.

In practice, the original Portage model has proved itself to be remarkably robust. Components like *criterion-referenced assessment* using the Portage checklist (Bluma *et al.*, 1976), the use of *activity charts*, continuous *monitoring* and *record keeping* survive almost unchanged from the original project which was developed in the early 1970s in Portage, Wisconsin (Shearer and Shearer, 1972).

There has however been one other unusual aspect of the Portage approach. The self-evaluation component has ensured that Portage became a dynamic (as opposed to static) model which attempted not only to *maintain* but to *improve* service delivery. As a result, people working within Portage have both added to the original service delivery model and expanded the Portage technology into new problem areas (see Cameron, 1984c). In the remainder of this chapter, four areas of future development will be discussed. These are:

(a) Portage and non-educational problems
(b) Portage and profoundly handicapped children
(c) Portage and the teaching of early communication skills
(d) Portage and the quality of learning.

Non-educational problems

Portage needs to help parents with *their* difficulties as well as the children's (Russell, 1985).

Perhaps we will never cease to care that our child is retarded (Philps, 1984).

In recommending the Portage service to other families with a handicapped child, parents have been at pains to stress the value of the practical help which they have received. However, they have additionally highlighted the fact that home teachers have helped them to tackle non-educational problems especially family problems (see Smith *et al.* (1977), Revill and Blunden (1979a) for details). It is clear therefore that parents can benefit from the home teaching component and the help with family problems which a regularly visiting home teacher can provide (Holland and Noaks (1982), J. Cameron (1984)).

The need to extend the Portage methodology to include non-educational problems which occur within the family as a whole has been increasingly recognized by existing Portage services and has been vigorously championed by an enthusiastic group within the National Portage Association (see especially Dessent (1984), Buckley (1984), Le Poidevin and Cameron (1985)).

Suggestions on how the existing Portage model can be developed to help parents to deal with family problems, have come from what are usually seen as two differing support systems – *Bereavement Counselling* and *Behavioural Psychology*. These two methodologies have been summarized in Figure 1 and despite the fact that they stem from quite different approaches to helping clients to deal with problems, the similarities in application are quite striking.

Indeed, the possibility of combining the two approaches holds a number of attractions. In particular, the behaviourally orientated problem centred approach could gain from some of the subtle techniques in problem identification and clarification suggested by Le Poidevin (1986) while the counselling model could be improved by some of the well-established techniques in applied behaviour

Bereavement Counselling Approach (After Le Poidevin, 1986)		*Problem Centred Approach* (After Cameron, 1985a)	
Step 1	Opening	Step 1	Assets and problem clarification
2	Getting the story	2	Selecting priorities
3	Summarizing themes	3	Examining controlling conditions
4	Setting goals	4	Setting objectives
5	Making the counselling contract	5	Agreeing strategy for change
6	Working through adjustment	6	Monitoring strategy for change
7	Evaluating outcome	7	Evaluating outcome
8	Closing	8	Renegotiating service delivery

Figure 1:   A comparison of two models for helping families to tackle non-educational/family   problems: (a)   the   Bereavement   Counselling Approach and (b)   the Problem Centred Approach

analysis developed to clarify the context in which problems occur and the strategies to enable clients to change their current responses to problem situations (see Cameron (1985a) for details).

When this interchange has been successfully completed, and when home teachers have been taught to use this approach successfully with parents, the Portage model will have received its most valuable addition to date. There is still a long way to go before Portage home teachers and parents can systematically tackle complex family problems but the early signs are promising!

Profoundly handicapped children

The difficulties of teaching profoundly handicapped children are well documented in the research literature and more recently some of the difficulties in using the Portage approach with such children have begun to emerge. Barna *et al.* (1980) reporting on the encouraging progress made by most children receiving the Portage home teaching service, mentioned that children with cerebral palsy and the visually handicapped group tended to develop at a very slow rate. Similarly, Bidder *et al.* (1982) noted that severely delayed children on their Portage scheme made fewest gains on the checklist. An even more depressing result was obtained by Felce *et al.* (1984) who found scarcely any evidence of skill acquisition in a group of profoundly handicapped adults in residential care who had received a modified Portage service.

This rather bleak picture which highlights the difficulties of teaching very severely and often multiply handicapped children is relieved a little by a number of recent initiatives which although still in their embryonic stages do offer exciting possibilities for this group. Such developments have occurred in the fields of curriculum planning, teaching method, assessment and evaluation and each of these is now discussed:

(a)   CURRICULUM PLANNING

Dessent and Ferguson (1984) have produced a comprehensive list of early teaching objectives in their checklist for the multiply handicapped. Although the task of *selecting* appropriate objectives for profoundly handicapped children remains a difficult one, materials such as these will aid this process and represent a useful downward extension of the original Portage checklist (Bluma *et al.*, *op. cit.*).

(b)   TEACHING METHOD

The Portage activity chart is a highly sophisticated teaching method. These charts have a remarkably high success rate (Shearer and Shearer, *op. cit.*, Revill and Blunden (1978), Castillo *et al.* (1982)), but further improvements appear possible.

Much work is going on at present to clarify the essential variables in *teaching* the profoundly handicapped. Such research includes the presentation of materials in discrimination tasks (Remington *et al.*, 1981) and the selective use of rewards (Olenick and Pear, 1980). Pioneering work is also going on in developing *management* techniques for highly disruptive behaviour (Kushlick *et al.* (1985), Lovass (1985)). These studies have shown how it is possible to decrease disruptive behaviour and to replace this with useful appropriate new skills.

All of these research developments could be incorporated into a Portage activity chart to improve the effectiveness of teaching the profoundly handicapped child.

(c)   ASSESSMENT

The Portage activity chart generates two pieces of assessment data – whether the learner carried out the response: (a) without help or (b) with help. For children who find great difficulty in learning, it may be important also to examine the *quality* of the desired behaviour.

As yet Portage does not have any systematic way of closely scrutinizing the performance of the learner. Such a device is however readily available in the Education of the Developmentally Young materials (EDY) developed at the University of Manchester (Foxen and McBrien, 1981) where the 'Qualitative Behaviour Record Schedule' could easily be adapted for home teachers and parents on a Portage scheme.

(d) EVALUATION

Another great strength of the EDY approach is that it allows the teacher to evaluate his or her performance using a 'Trainee Assessment Form'. Systematic feedback of this type has tended to get overlooked on Portage yet when teaching profoundly handicapped children the performance of the teacher is a crucial element in the learning equation. Once again, the trainee assessment form could easily be adapted for use on a home visit and would provide parents and home teachers with the kind of data which would enable them to teach even more effectively.

The development of new criterion-referenced checklist materials and continued research into the finer aspects of teaching method are encouraging developments within the existing Portage model. At the same time the EDY approaches to providing feedback on both the performance of the learner and the teacher could provide exciting new extensions to the existing Portage model (see Figure 2). Considering the degree of overlap which exists between Portage and EDY, it is scarcely surprising that 'the case for an arranged marriage' has been strongly made (see Stratford and Coyne (1986) for a stimulating discussion of this possibility).

Early communication skills

Although the Portage approach has been successfully used to stimulate early language development, the selection and teaching of early language skills demands considerable care and these are tasks in which most home teachers are likely to want to involve other supporting professionals particularly speech therapists. Recent research has begun to identify some specific problems in acquiring communication skills faced by children who have moderate and severe learning difficulties.

There are two major problem areas. In the first place, a number of researchers, notably Butterworth (1984), Dunst *et al.* (1982), Smith (1983) have reported that many handicapped children have *specific difficulties* in acquiring general communication skills, particularly imitation behaviours. A second problem concerns the parents of handicapped children. There are some indications that parents may use *functionally different language* towards their handicapped child (Cardoso-Martins and Mervis, 1985) and are less likely to follow the child's initiative (Jones, 1980). A modest study reported by Vicary (1985) suggested that Portage parents tended (initially at least) to use more directive speech to their children than other parents of handicapped children.

These research findings lead us to ask two questions.

(a)   Can children with special needs be helped via a Portage home teaching service to overcome some of their specific learning difficulties in early communication?

(b)   Can Portage help parents of handicapped children to respond more appropriately to their child's developmental level in language?

At present neither of these questions has been answered satisfactorily but there are some promising initiatives already occurring in Portage. In 1983 White and East produced their revised version of the language section of the Portage checklist. *The Wessex Revised Portage Checklist* offers a number of advantages for both parents and children. A section on *adult behaviour* ensures that the parent can respond appropriately to the child's level of language and provide the child with opportunities to develop existing language skills. As far as the child is concerned, the new checklist represents a considerably extended version of the original so that the selection of appropriate skills for teaching becomes easier. Many of these additional items fall into the category of *vocal and gestural imitation* which are precisely the specific deficit areas highlighted by research.

An important piece of additional research needs to be carried out to determine whether the *finer grained objectives for children* together with the *more appropriate adult behaviours* produce a significant improvement in children's early communication skills. At this stage, the possibility seems highly promising!

The quality of learning

The criteria for writing activity charts are so precise that the outcome of the parents' teaching is almost doomed to success (Cameron, 1979).

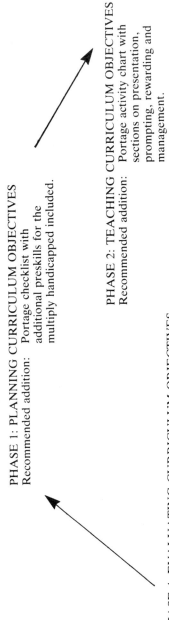

PHASE 1: PLANNING CURRICULUM OBJECTIVES
Recommended addition: Portage checklist with additional preskills for the multiply handicapped included.

PHASE 2: TEACHING CURRICULUM OBJECTIVES
Recommended addition: Portage activity chart with sections on presentation, prompting, rewarding and management.

PHASE 4: EVALUATING CURRICULUM OBJECTIVES
Recommended addition: EDY trainee assessment form to be used for evaluating the performance of the teacher in the teaching situation.

PHASE 3: ASSESSING CURRICULUM OBJECTIVES
Recommended addition: EDY qualitative behaviour record schedule to be used for assessing the performance of the learner in the teaching situation.

Figure 2: A model of Curriculum Management (after Lister and Cameron, 1986) showing how features of the Portage home teaching model and the Education of the Developmentally Young project might be combined to produce an improved service for profoundly handicapped children.

We find the assumptions and principles of learning by Portage incompatible with the present knowledge of how children learn . . . our task is therefore to find means whereby a child can be supported in his/her own search for understanding (Smith, 1984).

Although most people working in the field of education would find difficulty in dèfining the end results of teaching, many would agree that teaching outcomes involved helping the learner not only to *acquire* but to *apply* what has been learned. Learning can therefore be viewed as 'the ability to perform new skills in progressively more complex situations' (Haring *et al.*, 1978).

Recently, a number of writers (notably Hewson *et al.* (1980), McConkey (1981), Smith (1983, 1984)) have posed the question: *do highly structured behavioural approaches like Portage lead to high quality learning on the part of the child?*

Unfortunately, as yet there is no conclusive evidence from work carried out with pre-school handicapped children which we can use to resolve this question. However an attempt can be made to clarify the situation by examining the data from the US 'Follow Through' project. This large-scale research project was aimed at reducing school failure among economically disadvantaged pupils and a total of 75,000 children in 170 communities took part, with more than 20 different teaching approaches being tried out.

An independent evaluation of nine of these teaching approaches (reported in Becker *et al.*, 1981) produced results which were both clear cut and convincing. Not only, as everyone expected, did the most structured approach (Direct Instruction) succeed best of all in teaching *basic skills* to children but (contrary to what was expected) the children on the DI programme were able to use these skills more effectively than any other group *to solve new problems.* In addition positive change occurred in the way in which children on the DI programme viewed themselves as individuals. In short, the Direct Instructional approach out-performed all the other teaching methods in terms of teaching basic skills, helping children to develop problem solving strategies and improving their self-esteem.

While the results of this large-scale study are most encouraging for people working within the Portage model, it is important to guard against complacency. As has been strongly argued at the Second National Portage Conference in Cambridge (Cameron,

1984b) the elements for ensuring that children *maintain, generalize* and *adapt* the skills they have been taught on a teaching programme should always be built into the teaching programme. In particular, generalization and adaptation should not merely be expected to occur naturally. Fortunately, in the Portage scheme, many features which lead to maintenance, generalization and adaptation are already built into the model but some additional suggestions are made in the Cameron (*op. cit.*) paper.

One of the most important strategies for encouraging high quality learning was described by White (1986) at the Fourth National Portage Conference. She stressed the importance of *structured play* in helping children with special needs to maintain, generalize and adapt the skills they have been taught. Interestingly enough, the importance of structured play in teaching is also stressed by a number of people working within the cognitive model including Hewson *et al.* (1980), McConkey (1981) and Smith (1984).

Encouraging high quality learning is a future research growth area and because the Portage teaching approach has such solid foundations it can be easily built upon. Once again, a modest beginning has already been made!

Conclusion

The four topics which have taken up most of the content of this chapter are of course relatively new and only briefly touched upon in basic Portage training workshops. The need for an advanced Portage workshop for experienced Portage home teachers, supervisors and parents has been highlighted (Daly, 1984) and these topics – dealing with non-educational problems, teaching the profoundly handicapped child, teaching early communication skills and helping children to generalize and adapt taught skills – are likely to form the major part of this advanced curriculum.

It is also clear from the points raised in this chapter that Portage has not merely acted as an exemplary service but has also developed and expanded into new problem areas and as a result has both stimulated research and identified new areas for future investigation. All of these have been used to improve and strengthen the original home teaching model.

CHAPTER 8
Some Ethical Problems in the Practice of Portage

Sandra Stevens

Sandra Stevens is a Senior Clinical Psychologist in Ipswich, and is joint supervisor of the Suffolk Portage Scheme (East) and Chairperson of the Ethics Committee of the National Portage Association.

During the last two years, the Ethics Committee of the National Portage Association has been concerned with drawing up ethical guidelines for home visitors and other people involved in the delivery of Portage.

What is an ethical code?

Inevitably, ethics is concerned with the 'rightness' or 'wrongness' of actions and, therefore, what actions are 'desirable' and what are 'undesirable'. It is recognized that, in the context of Portage, decisions as to the desirability or undesirability of an act are necessarily subjectively determined, as opposed to those acts which may be seen as having an intrinsic or absolute rightness or wrongness. (We have only to look at historical and cultural differences in child-rearing practices to acknowledge that what is desirable in one society is frowned upon in another. Within any one society, groups and individuals differ in what behaviour they regard as desirable and what behaviour they feel should be discouraged (Blumenfeld, 1974).)

What has the Ethics Committee been attempting when drawing up an ethical code? We have suggested guidelines as to what actions we consider 'morally right' in our carrying out of the Portage model. In no sense do we see our deliberations as final or immutable. We expect, and hope, that the guidelines will change in response to being put to the test of aiding the solution of various problems which we anticipate will be brought to the Ethics Committee.

It could be argued that, because no two families or two children are alike, every situation in which the home visitor finds herself/ himself is unique, and therefore no general ethical principles of action can apply. However, in practice it is quite clear that there are many problems which occur regularly and which demand similar deliberations. In our ethical guidelines we are, it is hoped, providing (at the very least) a framework within which problems can be considered. Obviously 'guidelines' can only guide, they cannot determine: each person involved in Portage still has to make the ultimate decision as to the rightness or wrongness of his or her actions.

Why have an ethical code?

It has been asked, quite justifiably, why such a code is necessary: after all, not even all professional groups involved in the care and welfare of children have found it necessary to have ethical codes. Is it not an intrinsic part of our involvement that we have as our central tenet the welfare of the children involved and is this not in itself sufficient to ensure we act in a morally sound way? No one would dispute that the central principle of our work in Portage is the goal of achieving the greatest possible happiness for the children with whom we are involved. Indeed, the preamble to the draft guidelines is as follows:

> Members of the National Portage Association respect the dignity, individuality and the worth of each person and reject the belief that a person's worth and rights depend upon his or her competence or success.
> Members are aware of the position of great privilege they occupy in being allowed to assist in promoting the development of children and therefore will constantly endeavour to use their abilities and skills to the children's best interests.

Why then do we need ethical guidelines? The role of the home visitor is to fulfil two broad major functions. The first is that of helping the parents teach their children using behavioural techniques. The second function, one which parents have rightly forced us to recognize, is that of being involved in giving the family emotional support and aiding them in their adaptation to their child's handicap. Both of these aspects of our work involve decisions which have important consequences for the happiness of a child. As Leon Eisenberg has succinctly put it, 'It is the existence of choices that makes a difference that heightens ethical responsibility. Advice without consequences poses no dilemmas' (Eisenberg, 1975). Both these aforementioned functions, therefore, involve ethical considerations which we cannot ignore.

Ethical problems and behavioural techniques

We cannot escape the fact that behavioural procedures are often viewed with anxiety and suspicion by the public at large (Bandura, 1975) and that the very mention of the word 'reinforcement' can be enough to result in the condemnation of the procedures involved!

Such attitudes deny the very real role that behavioural methods can play in enhancing the lives of participants. Nevertheless, it would be foolish to ignore the great *potential for misuse* of behavioural methods and the need, therefore, for guidelines. An example of the acceptance of such a need was the publication in 1980 in Britain of a 'Report of a Joint Working Party to Formulate Ethical Guidelines for the Conduct of Programmes of Behavioural Modification in the National Health Service', which considered the formation of Behaviour Modification Review Committees throughout the country. In America there has been much unease and debate about the role of behaviour modification programmes in institutions, and courts have been involved in ensuring that 'treatment programmes do not violate the constitutional rights of participants', and have outlined appropriate safeguards (May *et al.*, 1974).

Karasu (1981) summarizes some of the ethical problems to be considered by anyone using behavioural techniques in saying that 'he has to grapple with additional ethical problems arising out of his unique philosophy and techniques: namely, to his molecular (but perhaps dehumanising) view of men and psychopathology; his specific (but perhaps reductionist) goals in treatment; and his efficient and precise (but perhaps aversive, coercive, mechanical and materialistic) methods'.

More specifically, Portage itself has been criticized for teaching discrete skills, without relating these skills to the child's cognitive development (Cunningham, 1982). Those of us in Portage would strongly deny any such charges of a mechanistic approach (Cameron, 1984b), and would join with those who would call such approaches unethical. *To some extent we must also acknowledge that we have brought such criticisms upon ourselves by failing to stress that the proper practice of Portage involves a good understanding of child development and a great sensitivity to the behaviour of the child, an ability to analyse that behaviour within the context of the family and the child's wider environment.* Such an approach, taking cues from the child, enables us to combine high precision teaching with an holistic approach to the child. In the guidelines the Ethics Committee has tried to guard against any 'dehumanizing' approach by outlining standards of intervention for the teaching of skills and for the management of unwanted behaviour. We have stressed the need for 'adequate individual and educational intervention planned to build individual skills, respectful of the child's dignity and freedom of choice' and have covered, for example, the need to ensure that skills are generalized and maintained. One parent of a multi-handicapped child, after a week of hospital visits, welcomed her Portage home teacher with the words: 'It's such a relief to see you. You really see "Chris" as a whole child; not just as eyes which aren't functioning properly and limbs which don't work.' That is not the comment of a parent who feels that her child has been subjected to 'mechanical methods'.

Dealing with 'unwanted' behaviour

Although in the general area of skill acquisition we can discount many of the criticisms made against behaviour modification techniques in Portage, nevertheless, in dealing with unwanted behaviours, such as non-compliant, disruptive or mutilating behaviour, then the behaviour modification approach does lead to different ethical problems to which we must address ourselves. However, if we maintain as pre-eminent the needs of the child and are guided by the consideration of what will lead to the child's greatest happiness, then most problems in practice become amenable to analysis and then to solution. We must acknowledge that procedures concerned with changing behaviour are based on value judgements. We must also acknowledge that we are manipulating behaviour.

However, it must also be realized that parents, without our intervention, attempt to manipulate their child's behaviour, attempt to decrease the 'unwanted' behaviours their child shows. All we are doing is helping them to deal with these problems more effectively, *often using less drastic, more positive measures than they might have done without guidance.* Nevertheless, the term 'unwanted behaviour' does have social connotations. We must ensure that the so-called unwanted behaviour is not labelled as such solely because it does not conform to the behaviour desired by parents or teachers. We have to make a subjective judgement that the unwanted behaviour is detrimental to the well-being of the child or is detrimental to the well-being of the other members of his or her family (and would be considered intolerable by most families). There are no absolute rights and wrongs in such cases, and one has obviously to exercise judgement. We have tried in the guidelines, however, to give guidance as to good practice in making these judgements and have given specific guidance about the implementation of programmes to deal with unwanted behaviour. We begin by stressing that these should not involve any avoidable physical or psychological discomfort, and acknowledge the need for the most stringent of safeguards by specifying that no intervention will take place without a detailed discussion of the problem at a staff meeting, and that any doubts as to its ethical standing should be referred to the Ethics Committee. We also say, unequivocally, that no intervention will take place without a frequent and thorough review of progress with the team supervisor at each supervisory session. It should be remembered that these safeguards are required for all procedures dealing with unwanted behaviours and are recommended even for such commonly recurring problems as temper tantrums. Also we have attempted to draw up a hierarchy of techniques so that there is guidance as to what techniques may be used and in what order they should be tried.

Ethical considerations and emotional support

The other aspect of our work, that of providing emotional support, also has important ethical considerations. Those of us involved in Portage, both parents and home visitors, acknowledge a very deep level of commitment and mutual trust which is often greater than that found in other professional–client relationships. A result of this trust is that the home visitor is in fact often in a position of great influence within the family: it is essential that this is recognized and that the home visitor takes steps to ensure that she or he is sensitive to the needs of the family and is prepared, above all, to listen to their views, to their anxieties, and then to aid them in finding appropriate agencies to help with problems.

The home visitor must be prepared to act as the family's and child's advocate in situations where there is such a need. Parents are usually the best advocates of their own child's interests, but this is not always the case, and then the situation occurs where the home visitor is caught in a conflict between loyalty to the family and the knowledge that the child's best interests are not being served.

An example of such a situation is a recent case in which a home visitor was the only person allowed into a home and where she had managed to build up a relationship of considerable mutual trust and care within the family. It became gradually apparent, however, that one child was at risk within the family, even though the other children were well cared for and were thriving. Here it was obviously necessary to break confidentiality with the parents and disclose information and views which supported the child's needs rather than those of the parents.

Although, ultimately, the home visitor's conduct will be dependent upon what is felt to be morally appropriate, we have tried in the guidelines to give general guidance on action in such cases. Home teachers are recommended to seek the aid of the supervisor or management team, and also to refer the problem to the Ethics Committee if the right course of action is difficult to determine.

Honest opinion

The recognition of the home visitor's influence within the family
demands a heightened awareness of the need to deal with the family
with complete honesty. Although at first sight such a stipulation
might seem unnecessary because of the unlikelihood of a home
visitor deliberately misleading parents, nevertheless, the very
laudable concern felt for the family might in itself lead to the home
visitor succumbing to the temptations of misguidedly presenting the
child's abilities in an unduly advantageous light, thereby painting an
over-optimistic picture of the child's potential and creating unreal
parental expectations. There is often a very fine dividing line
between *well-founded encouraging optimism and the folly of undue
overestimation* of the child's abilities: the former leads to a happy
outcome for the child and family, the latter to disappointment and
dejection.

An allied problem occurs when a home teacher is asked for a
definitive prediction of outcome for the child. Although prognosis
is not really within the terms of reference of a home visitor, it would
be ingenuous not to accept that, by virtue of the depth of
involvement with the family and concern for the child's progress, a
home teacher can be drawn into a discussion of the child's
'potential'. Often the only honest response, particularly in
considering multiply handicapped children, is that the home visitor
'does not know', but it is primarily this response which parents find
most difficult to accept.

All those involved in the care of young children with special needs
know the understandable pressures some parents exert to be given a
definite prognosis. They have also experienced the detrimental
effect of wrong predictions on the parents' outlook and the child's
developments. What is being advocated, of course, is not the blank
refusal to be drawn into discussion. Perhaps the most helpful way to
tackle the problem is by discussing how interrelationships between
specific handicaps make predictions difficult, i.e. how, for example,
a physically handicapped child's experience is limited by the
inability to explore freely and therefore might lead to his or her
being unable to acquire skills which do not seem at first sight to be
linked to physical disability. Where prognosis is difficult the stress
must be on 'keeping an open mind'. Nevertheless, it has to be
admitted that we must not underestimate just how difficult this area
is for both parents and home visitors.

Confidentiality

The example, previously cited, raises problems, not just of conflict of interest but also of confidentiality. The issue of confidentiality is one which rarely in practice poses problems in the practice of Portage, but the Portage home visitor, in the child's best interests, has to liaise with people from many different professions, and therefore this is an area which is potentially problematic and demands guidelines. All information received within the family is deemed confidential: yet confidential information might lead a home visitor to feel that action is needed and that there is a need to discuss the problem at a staff meeting or with other professionals. What happens, for example, if a home visitor suspects that a parent is 'clinically depressed' and needs help, but at the same time does not know what action to take? It would be inhumane not to attempt to help, but how does one do this without breaking confidentiality?

As a general rule, one safeguard is to make it clear to the family at the beginning of Portage intervention that there is a regular staff meeting at which the child's progress and problems will be discussed unless the parents have specifically asked for an item to be kept confidential. Thus, it is made clear to the parents that the home visitor will usually disclose information to Portage colleagues. Nevertheless, if any particularly sensitive information is received during a Portage visit, then the home visitor should take the extra precaution of obtaining the permission of the parent before disclosing this at a staff meeting. *Of course, if a parent expressly states that information is confidential, then the only grounds for breaking such confidentiality would be if the child, or anyone else in the family, was in danger or if the information related to a criminal act.* In most instances, however, problems such as these do not arise because most parents are very grateful to be able to discuss their problems with the home visitor and will respond willingly to suggestions that the home visitor should seek further advice on their behalf.

On the more routine matter of reports of the children's progress, again problems of confidentiality can arise. Though it is incumbent upon the home visitor to make sure that other professionals involved in the child's development are kept informed of his or her progress, it is a simple precaution and one adopted without problem by many Portage schemes, to check with the parents what information they want recorded and the list of people to whom that information should be circulated. If we are truly working 'in partnership' with parents, then it is difficult to avoid the conclusion that such action must be taken, and we have therefore incorporated this in the guidelines.

Ethical considerations: service delivery

One sometimes hears comments about Portage, such as 'and, after all, even if we don't achieve much by our intervention, we can't do any harm'. Such comments are not only wrong, but demonstrate a lack of understanding of the power of Portage intervention, a power which we must recognize, must be constantly aware of, and which we must subject to the strictest discipline. This becomes particularly important when we consider the partnership aspect of Portage. In regarding parents and home visitors as working in partnership, we are rejecting the paternalism common in the practice of many of the caring professions (Barnett, 1985). We must accept the fact, however, that in rejecting such paternalism we are also rejecting the professional's primary responsibility for the child's progress and are underlining the all-embracing responsibility that parents have in deciding the best course of action for their child. Partnership means that, in addition to successes being shared, failures are also shared!

The very fact of working in partnership with parents increases our responsibility, therefore, to make sure that the interventions are of the highest standards. We cannot, and must not, be responsible for increasing any family's sense of failure and incompetence by allowing poor standards of intervention. That is not to say, of course, that if we fail to succeed in the goals we have set, we have behaved unethically. We obviously will make mistakes, will make wrong judgements and then will fail. Indeed, the more ambitious the goals set the more likelihood there is of progress and of failure, and it is certainly not being advocated that the fear of failure should deter our trying to achieve difficult goals! What we must not do is fail through avoidable, general incompetence, or negligence.

We can take steps to decrease the likelihood of incompetent practice, first, by ensuring adequate training and, secondly, by then taking steps to remain competent by keeping abreast of new developments and research findings. Both these requisites are incorporated in the ethical guidelines.

What happens, however, when, in spite of these precautions, a home visitor is generally incompetent? Does that incompetence have any ethical connotations? If a home visitor knows him or herself to be incompetent, either through lack of expertise or through illness or emotional trauma, such a person is, we feel, morally bound to organize the termination of involvement with a family. If other colleagues, however, recognize the incompetence, then we feel it is up to those colleagues to take appropriate steps to ensure that involvement is either improved or terminated. This duty, of course, falls particularly upon the supervisor of projects, and we suggest in the guidelines that at first informal steps should be taken to solve the problem, but if these informal steps fail, then more formal action must be taken. Similarly, if the home visitor acts in a negligent way – not keeping appointments, for example, or keeping inadequate records – then, again, steps must be taken to terminate involvement. *On no account, can we allow a family involved in Portage to suffer the extra stress of poor Portage intervention!*

Caring for the home teacher

Some problems referred to the Ethics Committee have reflected concerns we had not anticipated having to incorporate in the guidelines; that is, problems reflecting the rightly-felt concern of supervisors for the well-being of home visitors. For example, questions were asked about the 'rightness' of expecting a home visitor to work in an extremely insanitary house, or to provide help for a severely handicapped child, not because the intervention might be unsuited to the child's needs, but because it might prove unacceptably stressful for the home visitor. (In both of these examples the Committee was in no doubt that Portage intervention should be offered, but recommended procedures for providing the home visitor with the extra guidance and support in recognition of the stress she or he might feel.)

It is usually assumed that within the caring professions the structure of management is reflected in a parallel structure of care, but some of the child abuse cases reported in the press would give the lie to that assumption and would seem to indicate a need for some measure of protection for the carer against exploitation and too much stress. Most Portage interventions result in the home visitor experiencing good friendship and joy: sometimes, however, the intervention poses considerable strain and then it is necessary to provide extra support and even be prepared to remove him or her should the strain become too great. We would suggest that the pyramidal structure of management found in most Portage schemes should be reflected in a comparable pyramidal structure of *care*, and that the management teams must take the ultimate responsibility for the well-being of all personnel involved in Portage.

Footnote

In all our attempts to compile the ethical guidelines, we have borne in mind the need to make them accessible to clients and diverse professional groups, both in terms of availability and in terms of the language in which they are written being understandable and jargon-free. Although we have paid great attention to the language of the guidelines and tried to eschew jargon, it proved unexpectedly difficult to combine precision with simplicity and clarity, and I am not sure we have achieved that goal.

The other drawback to compiling and writing about ethical guidelines is that of falling into the trap of sermonizing: when one is only too aware of one's own limitations, it is an unenviable task to have to write guidelines for the behaviour of others, and, however hard one tries, it is difficult to avoid a moralistic tone! For that we apologize.

We can only repeat that we expect the guidelines to change as their usefulness is put to the test and we hope that *all* participants will contribute to this process and help make them reflect what we all regard as 'morally right' in Portage.

CHAPTER 9
The Formation and Work of the National Portage Association

Dee Williams

Dee Williams is Chairperson of the National Portage Association.

In 1976 a new and powerful model of home teaching was introduced into the United Kingdom. The previous chapters have described the model in detail and given evidence of its successful implementation across the country, in a variety of settings and with different client populations.

When the first conference for Portage users was planned in 1981, the organizers were unprepared for the demand for places which followed the announcement of the event in the *Bulletin of the British Psychological Society* and the *Journal of the Association of Educational Psychologists*. It had been anticipated that some of the Wessex-trained Portage workers, then spreading the word in far-flung parts of the UK and beyond, would respond to the call. It was also hoped to capture the interest of a few others who had heard of the model and would welcome the opportunity for a more in-depth exploration of its potentialities.

The First National Conference

In the event the response was overwhelming, with many applicants being disappointed as the conference capacity was soon reached. Participants came from a wide geographical area and shared a wide range of success stories. Many variations to the original model had evolved as colleagues had come across the published Portage materials and read about the model in journal articles and adapted it to suit local needs. Although originated as a home teaching service to provide parents with the skills and support to teach their young child in the home, the Conference heard of successful adaptations within both residential and school settings. The client population covered a range from birth to adulthood and the 'parent' role was extended to care staff and teachers.

Common to all the schemes described at the Conference was the commitment of the workers involved and the evidence of benefit to the client populations. Despite their diversity, the essential components of the Portage model were being adhered to. In each case goals were negotiated between the service receiver and provider, teaching targets were precisely defined, the teaching activity was modelled, performance was recorded and the intervention was monitored. The Conference was a great success. The only complaint heard was that a choice had had to be made between very attractive alternative sessions. The general mood was celebratory, farewells were couched as 'au revoirs' and a date and venue agreed| for another conference the following year. (See Cameron (1982) for a summary of the Conference proceedings.)

The 1981 Conference had confirmed that Portage had become established as a service for families with developmentally delayed children. More than 30 projects had sent participants to it and all the contributors had spelled out the same message – Portage works. The robustness of the model had been tested by the various successful adaptations reported and plans for further developments to the model by the Wessex Health Care Evaluation Research Team had been outlined, subject to Department of Health and Social Security approval of funding (Glossop and Castillo, 1982).

The successful spread of Portage projects, however, had been largely dependent upon professionals from many different disciplines giving time voluntarily to act as supervisors and/or home visitors. Some were working in isolation without the support of a multi-disciplinary team and only a very few projects had funding.

The Second National Conference

In planning the Second Conference the organizers had decided that an additional element of criticism should be included to temper the celebration of the participants. Perhaps this was a mark of Portage 'coming of age'! There had been many reported evaluations (Smith *et al.* (1977), Revill and Blunden (1979a), Daly (1980), Cusworth (1980)). From the evidence available it appeared that parents could be taught to be successful teachers of their children; that structured precision teaching had enabled children to acquire a range of skills and that parents were very satisfied with the service they received through Portage. In voicing her concerns Sandow (1984) did not challenge any of these claims. Her criticisms were based on the possible inappropriate use of the materials by ill-informed and untrained persons. She also suggested that with some young children it would be necessary to establish the 'experience of pleasure' before reinforcers could be identified which could be used in the teaching of new skills and was concerned that this was not explained in the published materials.

The difficulty of identifying reinforcers for the population of profoundly handicapped children had been previously noted in the literature. Portage practitioners had also experienced this difficulty and a paper given at the same Conference (Dessent and Ferguson, 1984) describes working with two such children. A strength of the Portage model is the in-built support of the supervisory meeting. Team members share their collective experience/expertise to offer advice and suggestions on approaches which might be successful wherever a home visitor reports a difficulty. A key person at such meetings is the supervisor who would normally have had a training in behavioural psychology and a knowledge of the applied Portage model.

Sandow (*op. cit.*) also questioned the concept of partnership inherent in the Portage model. If the parent was the 'senior partner' then, she suggested, the professional was likely to face the dilemma of either collaborating in inappropriate goal setting or exerting pressure on the parent to accept his or her advice. In practice it has been found that a trusting relationship between parent and home visitor is established through working together. Each respects the knowledge and expertise of the other and joint planning of goals reflects this. The concept of seniority within this framework becomes irrelevant.

A final criticism focused on the appropriateness of some goals set and the time span allowed for achieving them. The purpose of the teaching is to enable the child to learn new skills in areas of deficit which will facilitate integration in the home and social settings. The selection of goals is guided by a developmental checklist but a specific goal will be chosen after a careful consideration of skills which it would be in the child's interest to acquire. The selection may not be scientific but it is based on practical, not arbitrary grounds. Experience had shown that weekly target setting was not always appropriate for the children with the most severe learning difficulties. However in the majority of cases task analysis of skills into very small steps enabled measurable progress to be monitored on a weekly basis. The suggestion that this was dangerous because parents may measure their own worth, and that of the child, by the outcome of the activity, was a hypothesis offered without supporting evidence.

The value of Sandow's contribution was that it pointed out the potential dangers of Portage materials being used by individuals without training and without the support of a supervisory structure. *The criticisms did not seem to be levelled at the model but rather at some possible applications of it.* It was interesting that concern to ensure high standards of service delivery which avoided the pitfalls identified by Sandow was shared by many Conference participants and was the subject of the seminar given by Albert Kushlick (1984).

Proposal for a National Association

It was obvious from the many presentations at both conferences, and the informal discussions among participants, that Portage had been adapted to suit a variety of local needs. In most cases practitioners were attempting to operate a 'service' which fulfilled most of the criteria of the Wessex model. However difficulties arose when there was no supervisory structure or support from statutory agencies at management level. Some colleagues had faced the disappointment of a project being closed down as a result of key personnel moving away from the area. It had also become clear to the more experienced Portage workers that the curriculum offered by the published materials was inadequate for some of the client population. Some modifications were already in process of being published (White and East, 1983) and others were being shared among colleagues at their supervisory meetings.

Additionally practitioners who had attended a basic training workshop were pointing out a need for advanced training. In particular it had ben noted that there was no formal training for supervisors. Concern was also expressed that service managers were seldom offered anything more than a brief introduction to the general principles and rationale of Portage. Over the six years since its introduction to the UK, Portage had taken root and was showing a healthy growth rate. However if this was to continue it was important that developments should be encouraged and monitored, both in styles of service delivery and curriculum activities. It was also important to identify unexpected and unplanned outcomes of parent enthusiasm and positive regard for their own teaching which affected other outcomes in their lives. Kushlick ended his seminar with the proposition that 'the Conference set up a Working Group whose members will meet over the next year and report on the possibilities of setting up a National Portage Association to the 1983 National Conference'. This was received enthusiastically and 15 participants volunteered to be members of such a group.

The working group deliberations

During the next year the working group met on ten occasions and I would like to express my thanks to all the members. Through their hard work and willingness to spend hours in debate identifying the factors which contributed to the effectiveness of a Portage service it was possible to present a comprehensive argument for the establishment of a national association at the next conference. The members of the working group were fairly representative of people involved in Portage. There were home visitors from a range of professional backgrounds, supervisors, parents receiving the service and researchers. The members were also involved in a variety of models of service delivery.

In examining the case for the establishment of a national association discussion focused on four main areas:

i) identifying the essential components of a service
ii) maintaining standards of service delivery
iii) establishing an information/support system for members
iv) financing the organization.

Identifying the essential components

Despite the varied backgrounds and Portage experiences shared by the working group members there was a general agreement that a major strength of the Portage model was its well-structured, task-orientated approach through which parents were taught direct teaching techniques which enabled them to help their child to acquire new skills. Parents were not passive receivers of a service but active partners. The recognition by the home visitor of the skills and expertise of the parents facilitated the collaborative model of parent and professional working together.

That was the easy part and it was agreed that the most accurate way in which to describe these components was to specify the performances which a home visitor would be expected to carry out. However it was generally felt that such a description failed to convey the importance of the parent–home visitor relationship and the many unexpected benefits which families receiving the service had reported experiencing, such as friendship and emotional support.

This was a critical area of discussion. Opinion was divided as to whether these outcomes were an essential component of the model or an additional benefit to be celebrated. It was important to explore these differences in perception and arrive at a consensus. There were many home visiting services available to parents with a developmentally delayed child. The parents receiving Portage had many times stressed that it was the regular visit and the practical help given by their home visitor in teaching them to teach their child which had made the service unique. Friendships often developed through the shared experience of celebrating the child's progress and planning activities to develop new skills. The one followed from the other. However it was also clear that Portage was effective even where the parent–home visitor relationship was limited to a working partnership. This was the crux. Agreement was finally reached. Additional positive outcomes, such as friendship and support, were a feature of the model but not an essential component of it. Recognition of this should be included in any description of the model.

Maintaining standards

The rapid growth of Portage services had confirmed the usefulness of the model as a tool for helping parents with young developmentally delayed children. Reported adaptations had demonstrated the dynamic nature of the model. However, concern had been expressed that the model could lose its precision and become attenuated in replication unless care was taken to ensure that the essential components were maintained and innovations were monitored for their effectiveness. There was also concern that the ready availability of the published materials could lead to services being established without the necessary training of personnel. It was felt important that parents being offered 'Portage' had a guarantee of a complete service, not the materials used in a different model of service delivery.

Three components were identified as being essential for maintaining standards of service delivery: training, monitoring and an ethical code of practice.

TRAINING

The working group agreed a core curriculum for the three-day initial workshop and offered a format for the training. This was an amalgam drawn from the pooled experience of those who had been involved in organizing training, including participants from the original workshop tutored by George Jesien of the Wisconsin Portage project. Consideration was also given to the need to develop advanced workshop curricula for experienced Portage workers.

The core curriculum content for a basic Portage workshop, lasting three to four days, is as follows:

(a)   The Portage model and materials
(b)   Problem identification and goal setting
(c)   Long-term curriculum planning
(d)   Writing activity charts
(e)   The home teaching process
(f)   Management of disruptive behaviour
(g)   Feedback and discussion.

MONITORING

Incorporated into the Portage model was a mechanism for service monitoring. The function of the supervisory meeting was to receive activity charts set by each home visitor, discuss their appropriateness and offer criticism within a supportive framework. The management team monitored the effectiveness of the service through the analysis of the activity chart data provided by the supervisor. In addition some services had requested information from parents, offering their views of the service they received. However there were also home visitors operating without any support structure and it was felt that a national association could have a role advising isolated members on strategies to enable them to establish a monitoring system. These might include inviting an educational psychologist or special educationalist to act as a consultant. Another alternative might be to send sample data to another service or to the national association.

An aspect of service delivery to which attention was drawn was inter-professional consultation. It was important to have effective channels through which to discuss a child's progress and future programmes with any professional involved with that child. This was an area in which some services had experienced difficulty and it was felt that it would be advantageous to have guidelines prepared by a national association to which members could refer.

AN ETHICAL CODE OF CONDUCT

Parents and home visitors often developed a special relationship over the period of Portage visits. Sometimes information was given which it was expected that the home visitor would treat as a confidence. There was a strong belief among the working group members that home visitors should always act in the interests of their families, and in particular the developmentally delayed child. Confidences should be respected unless the family had been told that it was considered necessary to share the information with a colleague or supervisor. It was recognized that this might occasionally face the home visitor with a conflict of interests and it was considered that a Code of Ethical Conduct could offer support and guidance in such situations.

It was also noted that home visitors sometimes have to offer advice to parents on ways of dealing with disruptive/destructive behaviours of the child. In rare instances the use of aversive techniques might be recommended and it was important that both parents and home visitor were aware of the ethical considerations involved in taking such a decision. A Code of Ethical Conduct would offer guidelines to members of an association. Such a code could also cover guidelines for researchers to ensure that the interests of the family were always safeguarded whenever they were part of a research project.

Establishing an information/support system

Participants at both conferences had found the opportunity to share experiences exciting and stimulating. There had been a sense of community created which had proved especially valuable to Portage workers in isolated services. However such events were being organized on an ad hoc basis and only a small percentage of practitioners were able to attend. A solution, proposed by the working group, was to have a regional structure within a national association. Regions could organize smaller events on a more regular basis and a network could be formed to keep members, and member services, in touch with each other. Inquiries from interested people could also be dealt with more efficiently at a regional level.

At national level, the association would have a role in promoting the model and seeking means of bringing the value of Portage to the public's attention. Existing services were scattered across the country but many had long waiting lists and there were still many areas where no services had been established. Parent receivers were enthusiastic about the value of Portage, but potential receivers could only seek the service if there was information about it readily available to them.

In addition to this proactive role, it was also felt that a watching brief should be kept on information about Portage which was being made available from other sources. Criticisms and challenges to the model should be responded to, to avoid misconceptions developing.

It was also strongly recommended that there should be a national newsletter provided for members to keep them informed of developments occurring in different parts of the country and to strengthen the sense of identity which had been forged by attendance at conference.

Financing the organization

The working group did not spend much time debating this issue. However it was obvious that any organization which was aiming to provide a service for its members would need financial resources. Sponsorship was considered as a means of obtaining funding and it was recommended that if the next conference agreed to the establishment of a national association, then charitable status should be applied for as soon as possible.

It was recognized that some funding would be required immediately in order to enable any member of the association standing for office to recoup expenses incurred through attending committee meetings. This was particularly important if parents were to be encouraged to participate in the association at all levels. Communication expenses would also need to be covered, such as postage of the newsletter, and it was strongly argued that financial assistance should be sought to enable more parents to attend the National Conference.

It was agreed that in the short term money was most likely to be obtained through membership subscriptions and donations.

Portage: home teaching or home visiting?

The working group report to the Third National Conference in London was unanimous in its recommendation to establish a national association. Papers were presented which outlined the proposed structure of the association, performances required of each of the committees and a skeleton code of practice for association members. None of these could be discussed in detail but they were accepted in principle as the foundation on which the association would be based. It was the recommendation relating to the name of the association which caused most debate. The main point of contention was whether the new association should be an umbrella organization encompassing any home visiting/teaching service or whether Portage was a special service fundamentally different from any other service available to families.

The point was crucial. Since 1976, Portage services had mushroomed across the country. A major reason for this success was that parents were given practical advice on how to help their child and were taught skills to enable them to carry out the teaching activities within a structured framework with regular feedback. They were equal partners in a collaborative effort to help the child. It was concern to ensure that this model of service delivery was maintained and that adaptations/innovations were adequately monitored that had guided the discussions of the working group.

An aim of the proposed association was to promote participation of all members of Portage services, both parents and Portage workers, in the evaluation of their service. Parents being offered Portage wanted to know what to expect and those in receipt of it could only evaluate the service if they knew the criteria against which to measure it.

The Portage model offered clear guidelines on the performances required of parents and home visitors, supervisors and members of the management team. If a code of practice for the association members was to be adopted, and this had been agreed in principle, it was important that it should apply to all members. It was recognized that in some instances small services and individuals might not be in a position to fulfil all the criteria in the short term. However agreement to work towards them seemed an important condition of membership.

The National Portage Association

The National Portage Association (NPA) was established in 1983 at the London Conference. The choice of name underlined the importance attached to maintaining the key components of the Portage model in the service delivered to parents. It also emphasized the centrality of the active role parents played in the service delivery. This is what makes Portage different!

The aims of the Association

Aim One: The Association will campaign for the setting up of services across the country so that any family with a developmentally delayed young child will have access to this support as one of a range of services available to them.

Aim Two: The Association will support its members and member services to maintain a high standard of service delivery by providing opportunities for relevant training at both initial and advanced levels. It will also develop a system of monitoring service delivery through the provision of a positive critical appraisal, linked with appropriate advice to registered services.

Aim Three: The Association will encourage developments and innovations in the service which accord with the overall principles of the model of service delivery and can be demonstrated to be in the interests of the client population.

Structure of the Association

The Association is structured on a two-tier model of regional and national representation. At both levels, elected officers are drawn from a wide range of practitioners including parents, home visitors and supervisors. Through them the Association is kept aware of the needs of its members and can plan its activities in response to them.

REGIONAL LEVEL

There are eight regions in the United Kingdom and each has an elected representative who is a member of the national committee. The regional representative is supported by a regional committee which is elected annually and must include some parent members. It was difficult to determine where to draw the boundaries for each region. Taking into account the need for members to have reasonable access to events organized within the region, the NPA adopted the structure of the prenationalized railway system as a guideline to its regional boundaries whilst leaving selection of regional membership to individuals. The eight regions are: Eastern, Ireland, London and South East, Midlands, Northern, Scotland,

South West and Wales.

Each region organizes a programme of events for its members and provides general information about known Portage services in their area. The regional representative is responsible for ensuring that members are kept informed of the activities of the Association and encouraging active participation in them.

NATIONAL LEVEL

At national level the Association has been concerned with promoting the Portage model of service delivery and providing support for existing practitioners. There are three nationally organized committees with responsibility for Training and Monitoring, Information, and Ethics. The chairperson of each is an elected member of the national committee. Other members of the national committee are the chairperson, secretary, treasurer and parent representatives.

Promoting new services

The National Survey of Portage Services carried out by the Wessex Health Care Evaluation Research Team (Bendall *et al.*, 1984) found that a large proportion were concentrated in the densely populated areas of London, the West Midlands, South Wales and Lancashire. In other areas, notably sparsely populated rural areas, there were very few services. One of the NPA's objectives, therefore, was to work towards bringing Portage into areas where there were no existing services.

The survey had also found that some services had been discontinued after a period of time and it considered possible reasons for this. Factors which appeared to contribute to closure of a service were lack of specific funding and /or a management team. It was therefore important in planning a campaign to extend Portage services to focus on a means of attracting support from the statutory local agencies and/or national government which could provide funding for them.

In 1983 Freddie Green, then Staff Inspector for Special Education at the Department of Education and Science (DES), became interested in the Portage model. He visited the Winchester service and participated in a basic workshop. With his support the NPA decided to work towards gaining recognition by the DES of the value of Portage as a pre-school service for developmentally delayed children. We were fortunate that the Secretary of State for Education took a personal interest in this development. It was the enthusiasm of the parents and their positive evaluation of the benefits gained through involvement with Portage which was influential in gaining his support. The structure of the model with its in-built positive monitoring system was another attractive feature as were the published evaluations of services which provided data about its effectiveness.

Educational support grant

In 1984 discussions were initiated between the DES and the NPA. The DES were interested in Portage and were considering including it in their educational support grant nominations. In this way local education authorities (LEAs) would be encouraged to set up services, initially supported by ESG monies. This would enable properly financed services to be established employing full-time Portage workers with administrative assistance and would eliminate one of the contra-factors to service continuation. The NPA shared the commitment to develop services across the country. However it was also concerned to maintain the features of the model which had contributed to its success.

Multi-agency involvement

One of these features was the involvement of all the statutory agencies concerned with providing services for pre-school handicapped children and their families. The initial research project had been funded by the Department of Health and Social Security. However a strength of the project had been the inclusion of representatives from education and social services on the management team. This had facilitated the development of an integrated service with effective use of existing resources. In their report the research team suggested that the service should be delivered '*jointly* by personnel from these agencies (i.e. the home teacher for a particular family will come from *either* health, education or social services)' (Smith *et al.*, 1977).

The follow-up survey (Bendall *et al.*, 1984) had found that multi-agency services had practical advantages over single-agency ones and were more likely to be sustained over time. This was partly because in such services many of the home visitors were carrying out Portage activities as part of their professional duties, the only difference being that their work with these families was systematized and supervised by the Portage supervisor.

Multi-disciplinary home visitor teams

Another advantageous feature of the model had been the multi-disciplinary composition of the home visitor team. Involvement of all agencies at management level encouraged staff from many disciplines to participate in the service either as front line workers or as consultants. This had given team members access to a wide range of skills which had better equipped them to deal with the many different problems which faced home visitors in the course of their duties. It also helped to ensure that targets worked on in the home were appropriate. The NPA was concerned to promote the inclusion of volunteer home visitors and seconded professionals drawn from other relevant disciplines in any new Portage service to support the full-time workers and enhance the quality of the service being offered to the families.

Evaluation

New services established under ESG funding would be guaranteed for three years. However if LEAs were to be persuaded to support their continuation after that time there would need to be evidence of their effectiveness. Experience has shown that an important contributory factor to existing services gaining funding had been an evaluation of the pilot stage of development. The system of setting written goals, record keeping and regular reporting to a management team offers tools and provides data for a systematic evaluation and the NPA strongly recommended that this should be built into the criteria for selection of proposals for services to be supported under ESG funding.

£1.2 million

Through the good offices of the DES and the canvassing efforts of the NPA, Portage was confirmed as a project to be supported through the 1986 ESG allocation. Funding of all approved services was for three years and it was recommended that applications could be submitted for three consecutive years, 1986–1988. The aim of the DES is to establish at least one model service in each LEA after which some may select to replicate the service according to their client population needs. The NPA was pleased to be invited to produce written guidelines for LEAs making application for funding (*A Guide to Setting up Portage Services*) and to organize an introductory workshop aimed at potential service managers.

Publicity and publications

The official recognition by the DES of the value of Portage to families with young developmentally delayed children has been a significant milestone in our history. However it is also important for information about the model to be shared on a much wider basis. Parents can only request the service if they know about it. Coverage by the media is an effective way of bringing Portage to the public's attention. The NPA has been successful in attracting the interest of local and national television producers. The television cameras have filmed in the homes of Portage families and the model has been promoted through this medium. There has also been a regular flow of articles submitted to both professional and popular publications which have aimed to keep Portage in the public eye and two parent members have shared the positive benefits they gained from receiving the service in books they have written about their children (Philps, 1984 and Lloyd, 1986).

Portage Post

In addition to spreading the word to the outside world, the NPA also has a responsibility for ensuring that its members are kept informed of events, training opportunities and news from other services. *Portage Post* is a termly publication which fulfils this function. Contributions are invited from any member and the national officers and regional representatives give a regular update on their activities.

In the future it is hoped that the NPA will develop its information service both as a reference facility and offering publications for sale. At the present time the production, collation and distribution of articles and publications depend on the voluntary efforts of its members and are restricted by the financial constraints of an organization operating on a shoe-string budget. Even so the *Guide to Setting up Portage Services,* the code of practice and the code of ethical conduct are now available and are a useful set of reference documents for anyone interested in being involved in Portage, either as a receiver or provider of the service.

NFER-Nelson and the NPA

When Portage was first introduced into this country, the published curriculum was also imported from the United States. This had been very advantageous in the early days of Portage and the 'little blue box' of teaching cards had become a trademark of the service. However, the Wisconsin project had been developed for families with mildly delayed children in a rural population who did not have access to any other pre-school facilities. In the UK Portage has been used with a much wider group of children, ranging from severe delay associated with intellectual and/or physical impairment through to mild developmental delay. It soon became obvious that the available curriculum was inadequate and many members were reporting on modified/supplementary materials which they were using. There was also a problem of terminology – American vocabulary was reported to be causing confusion to both parents and professionals alike.

NFER-Nelson are the publishing agents for Portage in the UK. They are interested in responding to the needs of the UK Portage users and have been working closely with the NPA to identify relevant areas for revision or additions to existing materials which would be helpful.

The Wessex Revised Portage Language Checklist (White and East, 1983) was the first British publication and negotiations are in hand for revising the cognitive, self-help and motor sections of the curriculum. The wider population with which Portage is used in the UK has also drawn attention to two notable omissions in the original published materials. The needs of the children with very severe/profound impairment and behaviour disorders had not been relevant to the US project. However it has become obvious that sections to cover both these groups of children must be included in the British version of the curriculum. Preliminary work on producing a curriculum for the children with multiple handicaps is already underway and the NPA has been fully supporting the recent work of Kushlick and the Wessex Health Care Education Research Team in developing an intervention package for children with severe behaviour difficulties (see Kushlick *et al.* (1985) for details). It is hoped that this will form a basis for a new 'Behaviour' section of the curriculum.

Initial and in-service training

To maintain high standards of service delivery it is vital for all Portage workers to have completed the basic workshop and to have demonstrated a satisfactory degree of competence on all components of the course. However one of the deficits of the original model was that the supervisor had no more formal training than a home visitor although the skills required of that person could not be covered in the basic workshop. It has also become clear that experienced Portage workers would benefit from advanced workshops at which aspects of their role could be considered in greater detail. This is an area in which the NPA is developing the services it can offer to its members.

The future

Since its establishment in September 1983 the NPA has taken significant steps towards achieving each of its objectives. Its success has depended upon the voluntary efforts of its committee members, past and present, and the enthusiastic support it has been given by its members. These efforts, in the immediacy of its establishment, have been concentrated on providing support for practitioners and demonstrating the value of such an organization. However it is now at a stage where it requires a sound financial basis. The importance of gaining financial support had been recognized by the original working group. An application has been made to the Charity Commissioners for recognition as a registered charity and an important goal in the near future is to attract sufficient funding to establish a central office, albeit a small room with an answering machine, administrative support and the appointment of at least one field officer.

The NPA has now gained official recognition. It has an important role to play in ensuring that Portage continues to meet the needs of its client population. This will be achieved through the active participation of parents within the Association at local, regional and national level. The NPA will also encourage developments in the service which will extend the help which can be given to families with a developmentally delayed child.

I would like to express my thanks to all members who have worked so hard to achieve this success and particularly to the members of the working group and the national committee for their support.

CHAPTER 10
Parental Involvement in the 1980s

Philippa Russell

Philippa Russell is Senior Officer, Voluntary Council for Handicapped Children, London.

The background to parental involvement

Recent government reports, from Plowden to Warnock, have highlighted the need for collaboration between parents and professionals. Since the 1967 Plowden Report, there have been various research studies which have demonstrated that over the past 15 years there has been a marked trend towards parental participation and parental presence in schools. The 1976 Court Report emphasized that it could see no better way to help children than to help their parents to share in their growth and development. The Taylor Report in turn proposed parental participation in school management and accountability. The Warnock Committee in 1978 saw parents and partnership as central themes in all their recommendations. Parents themselves have changing expectations of their rights and representation in education. Some of the Taylor Report's recommendations were implemented in the 1980 Education Act, ensuring that all maintained schools should now have parents as elected representatives on governing bodies. Hence parents have the opportunity to influence the curriculum and management within individual schools. The 1981 Education Act introduced accessibility of advice relating to a child's assessment for parents and gave parents formal rights to contribute to such an assessment, together with an appeals procedure for those who were dissatisfied with the outcome.

However, the right to partnership will not necessarily ensure that it happens. In the commercial sense of the word, partnership implies 'mutually profitable outcomes'. Some families will have earlier negative experiences of the education service (often from their own school days). Family illness, unemployment or pressure from other family members may create barriers. Whilst parents have clearly moved away from the dependent 'client' role, some will need active support in order to become partners.

When the Warnock Committee (1978) titled a key section of their report 'Parents as Partners', the Committee formally acknowledged the groundswell of government, professional and parental opinion that *parents* have a central role to play in their children's development and education. Traditionally parents have been perceived – implicitly or openly – as fulfilling a number of roles. They have been the object of study and research; have been consumers; can be innovators and finally, may be 'partners'. Partnership itself is open to many interpretations. Mittler (1979) has defined the essential characteristics as:

(i)   mutual respect and recognition of the essential equality between parents and professionals;

(ii)   the sharing of information and skills;

(iii) the sharing of feelings and perceptions;

(iv)   a shared process of decision making;

(v)   a recognition of respect for the individuality of families and individuality of the child.

Such characteristics could be merged into Wolfendale's (1985d) definition of 'partnership' as the 'equivalent expertise' of parent and professional.

Many parents have themselves queried what was meant by partnership. The concept could mean the facilitation of parents as good clients and passive participants in a professionally determined treatment programme. Conversely, parents as 'professionals' do not constitute a homogeneous group, but have their own professional training, code of practice and personal identity. If parents were to choose to be 'professionals', they would not only have to amalgamate a whole range of very different skills, but more importantly could lose the particular qualities which they bring to partnership by nature of being *parents*. Parents have a unique knowledge of their own child. They are passionately concerned for that child and an element of partiality is likely to encourage persistence, motivation and support where some more objective approaches may fail. Parents can learn many essential skills to make their knowledge accessible to professionals – but their availability and partiality may make them victims rather than partners if they are seen as a cheap and continuous treatment resource and if the needs of the whole family are not taken into account.

Partnership with parents will not always be comfortable for professionals. It may necessitate justifying professional decision making and sharing uncertainties. It will mean understanding why living with a difficulty may be very different to intervening on a one-off basis. It means understanding parental anxiety and depression, as well as sharing in successes. Dessent (1985) notes that 'parentology' has become the 'latest bandwagon within the profession of educational psychology'. Whilst parents do have a very special role, he argues that the shift to working with parents must be put in the *context of the family's own resources and abilities*. That is to say, partnership must be in the family's as well as the professional's own best interests. It will depend upon a genuine dialogue and respect for personal, cultural, educational and social differences within the individual family. It is not an expedient and cheap palliative for specific professional services, if these are required.

Partnership for the under-fives

The major legislative developments in forwarding partnership have focused upon the school setting. Yet it is certain that many parents are only 'partners' in the wider educational context, if they have learned to function as partners in the pre-school years. The Education Act 1981, for the first time in UK education legislation, introduced the concept of special educational provision literally from birth. The Act, a legal response to the Warnock Report, introduces a new broad concept of special education needs (abolishing the old formal categories of handicap and broadening the definition to include up to 18 per cent of the school population at any one time). Of central importance to the effective implementation of the Act, is the involvement of parents in assessment, with new rights not only to contribute to the 'statement of special educational needs', but to see the professional advice relating to the assessment.

The idea of 'special educational provision' for very young children developed in the 1960s, with growing involvement of educational and clinical psychologists in behaviour modification and other training programmes using parents as co-workers and, most importantly, with the formal recognition that the *family* was the most effective and economical system for fostering and sustaining the development of a young child. The early home visiting programmes were initiated in the USA (and subsequently widely developed in the United Kingdom). Such schemes had certain common and important features:

(a)   They were non-selective, including all families who wished to participate.

(b)   The partnership with the home visitor or teacher was seen as an integral part of the success of the programme – in terms of personal trust and relationships with other professionals.

(c)   Most programmes started by working with the child and going on to involve the parent (usually the mother).

(d)   Parental involvement was based on an initial agreement or contract setting out what the programme could offer and ensuring that demands on the parents were commensurate with other family or personal commitments.

(e)   Programmes taught *success* to parents who either felt inadequate or incompetent, or who were concerned that their child's special needs would inhibit progress. Demonstration, as well as written activities, was an integral part of such success.

The best known of the home teaching programmes is, of course, Portage and the scheme is now well established in the United Kingdom. Portage offers an invaluable strategy for involving parents in not only directly teaching their children new skills, but in assessing which skills should be selected and how success could be achieved. The Portage model involves professional support for the home teacher and has, equally importantly, given new skills to *professionals,* who frequently feel their lack of immediate practical help for families. Home teachers have included psychologists, health visitors, physiotherapists, volunteers, home liaison teachers and other people already working with a family. The flexibility of the programme enables parents to go as quickly as they and their child wish – and to begin literally from birth if appropriate.

Portage at its best offers parents the opportunity to understand the *principles behind any intervention* rather than offering, like a car care manual, recipes for tightening belts and guaranteeing better performance. As Elizabeth Newson* has often said, parents *are* experts on their child. They have a rich and unique knowledge of how that child functions and on abilities and disabilities. But they may not know how to organize that knowledge in a way which is directly relevant to helping the child. Indeed that knowledge *without* the help of a professional may actually hinder parents in helping the child, since it may appear depressing, confusing and hopeless.

The strength of Portage is as a means of assessment followed by action:

(i)   it *must* utilize what the parents already know;

(ii)   it *must* involve a caring and trained home visitor who is able to link back to a wider network of professionals;

(iii) it is a *private* service in as much as it can take place in a venue chosen by the parents. Successes and failure need not prematurely be displayed before a wide range of professionals who could be perceived as judging the parents;

---

*Co-director, Child Development Research Unit, University of Nottingham and joint author, with Tony Hipgrave, of *Getting through to your Handicapped Child* (1982).

(iv)   the parents can select priorities in their lives. *Educational goals* in terms of cognitive development may be less important (and indeed unattainable) unless the parents have first overcome *practical* problems like difficult behaviour;

(v)   the actual level of parental involvement can be matched to individual family dynamics. In the real world the mother of three pre-school children, living in poor housing and depressed by marital problems, is unlikely to be able to participate as actively as a young couple with few commitments, time, a good home environment, and an enthusiastic attitude to working with their child. *Portage, at its best, avoids overloading the system.* And, since it is home based, parents do not need to compare themselves to each other surreptitiously.

The Portage approach offers a flexible approach to helping children through their parents. It reinforces parental competence by teaching success. It also introduces parents to concepts of development which are applicable in a broader context, for example in ensuring parents' participation in the assessment procedures relating to the Education Act 1981.

Special parent, special child?

Successful parenting of a handicapped child will not only depend upon the recognition of the child's special needs because of the handicap, but upon the parents' ability to be competent, caring and confident parents to *any* child. Research by Wolkind and others at the London Hospital (1981) has clearly shown that many mothers suffer from depression when caring for young children. Whether such depression reflects problems of inner city living or greater (and perhaps unrealistic) expectations of parenthood in the 1980s, it clearly impairs mother/child relationships. Research has frequently demonstrated the extra burden placed upon many families when a child is handicapped. Ann Oakley (1974) has noted that all young children are demanding but that:

motherhood has a single long-term goal, which can be described as the mother's own eventual unemployment. A successful mother brings up her children to do without her.

Most handicapped children may be conspicuously delayed in reaching their developmental milestones. Basic living skills – like drinking from a cup, self-feeding or mobility – may be acquired late and only after intensive support. Although parents of any young child may feel temporarily trapped in routine care needs, parents of handicapped children may demonstrate such needs in a different dimension. A study of severely handicapped children and their families by the Family Fund (Glendenning, 1983) found that out of 361 children, 50.1 per cent could not be left alone for even ten minutes in a day. Wilkin's study (1979) of families of mentally handicapped children found that there was no evidence of significant help from relatives, friends or neighbours with problems of day-to-day caring. Indeed, Cunningham and Davis (1985b) and the Honeylands Progress Report (Brimblecombe, 1983) note that families and friends may – albeit inadvertently – reinforce the parents' perception of a child as 'different' and parental anxieties about both present and future development. Recognition of dimensions of care is important in planning support for families, since parental participation in educational programmes must in the end depend upon their ability to be involved in educational activities in the context of other demands made upon the family's time and energy.

Considerable evidence is amassing about the dissatisfaction experienced by many parents at the way in which the initial diagnosis of a handicap was made – and on the impact such dissatisfaction has on subsequent attitude to services. Cunningham and Davis (1985a) found 58 per cent of parents of Down's children dissatisfied with the initial diagnosis. A study in Kent by Pahl and Quine (1984) found that dissatisfaction was proportionately greater, the older the child was when a handicapping condition was diagnosed. Parents – particularly those with children with sensory handicaps – felt frustrated by months or years of inability to convince professionals that 'something was wrong' and frequently by the lack of immediate appropriate practical help after a later diagnosis to compensate for what was felt to be lost time. Cunningham and Davis (1985b), Brimblecombe (1983), and Pahl and Quine (*op. cit.*) all emphasized the considerable compensatory role of *immediate* practical help which would be available on a continuum basis; which would make sense of the complex inter-professional services which might be available; which would offer the parents a positive role in helping the child and which could offer a longer-term perspective about the child's development. Parents have always been clear that sentimentality has no place in support services, although sympathy and respect may be important ingredients in such services. The strength of the Portage model is that it can be tailored to individual needs; that it offers a focus for action and that it can provide a counselling element for families who may feel that their life has been turned upside-down and feel deskilled and inadequate as a result.

Research by Robin and Josser in France (1984) hypothesizes that all mothers develop a process of *anticipation* in interacting with their babies:

> Each mother has a plan for her child. It is a changeable plan, which is at the same time an interpretation of his behaviour and a projection into the future.

Robin and Josser argue that the child, as he or she matures, develops new characteristics which in turn restructure the child's image in the eyes of the parents. The mother learns from this interaction how to help the child on to the next stage of development. The concept of 'anticipation' is particularly relevant when a family has a 'special child'. Cunningham and Davis (1985a) have noted that parents begin to feel comfortable with the diagnosis of handicap in a child at different stages. Most parents will accomplish this within the 8th to 16th week after birth. Acceptance will often coincide with the child showing some normal infant behaviours such as making eye contact, smiling or taking pleasure in feeding. The child in effect becomes an individual and the parents may assert that the child is in fact no different to any other child and even develop over-optimistic expectations in terms of future development. However, from the ninth month onwards, the child's developmental gains may become slower. Doubts and concerns may re-emerge just as professional involvement begins to ease off towards the end of the first year of life. The child is in effect not meeting the 'life plan' stages envisaged by the parents. Help will be needed in re-orientating and setting acceptable patterns of anticipation. Positive expectations will need nurturing and families will be vulnerable without an *ongoing* programme of support.

An important part of partnership with parents (a concept which is frequently promoted but infrequently discussed in practice) must be assessing not only the immediate resources of the *professionals* to initiate a partnership, but the preferences as well as resources of the family. Tailoring models of partnership to what is available, rather than what is optimal, may be acceptable if the rationale is clearly spelled out as a short-term objective to family and to the professionals concerned. Parental partnership may take a variety of forms. Some services will be *centre* based, others like Portage private and *home* based. Workshops, adult education schemes or voluntary provision may offer other short-term options for parental involvement. Some options are compatible with each other (many Portage families using under-fives provision in a variety of contexts and being active in play and leisure schemes in the voluntary sector). Important factors in use, or non-use, of services will be the constraints of the family's own life style. One parent families working a traditional eight-hour day may simply not be available to participate in home-based learning services which cannot function in evenings or at weekends. Family illness, elderly dependents, poor housing or ill-health may inhibit regular involvement. McConachie (1983), looking at preferred patterns of involvement, makes the important distinction that 'some parents are very enthusiastic about teaching their own child in a structured way. Other parents want to pursue a more "natural" course of influencing their child and to leave teaching to teachers. Others may find consistent "special efforts" for the child difficult to sustain'. There is clear evidence that many families need support from a 'parent adviser' or 'named person' (see below) in order to become involved. The Honeylands 'home therapy' programme, which allocated 'home therapists' or 'named persons' to families of under-twos with special needs, found the availability of such a resource had a major impact on parental involvement and that 'poor motivation' or 'uninvolved' negative labels applied to some families were easily resolved in the identification and treatment for previously unidentified very real family difficulties.

Multi-professional approaches to working with parents

Special educational needs have become increasingly multi-professional. As the Fish Committee noted (1985), the new generation of parents suffer not from the isolation of the 1950s and 1960s, but increasingly from 'over-kill' and apparent duplication and fragmentation of services.

Problems between *professionals* must be clarified if parents are to participate. Problems in professional partnership may include:

(i)   The fact that many professionals and services working with children and families are still at different stages of their professional development.

(ii) Although each profession brings its own skills, there is some overlap in terms of concerns and roles.

(iii) Parental involvement will inevitably mean professionals having to publicly disagree and discuss issues in front of clients. Professionals are trained to negotiate. *Parents* will need training in order to see disagreement as part of a learning process about their child.

(iv) Confidentiality is more often a professional than a parental problem.

(v)   Professionals may themselves take broader or narrower views of their own roles.

Professionals involved with an individual family function in three broad areas. They may provide *treatment*; they may *refer* or they may work *cooperatively*. The latter may cause the greatest difficulty, since it implies accepting the complementary skills of *other* professionals. Where there are local complementary structures (such as child development or district handicap teams or Under-Fives Panels), such partnership may be relatively simple. But frequently parents feel victims of professional conspiracy or inaction, without awareness of professional dilemmas in working together.

Portage is primarily promoted as being a tool for *parental* involvement. However Portage offers a major resource for skill-training for *professionals* as well as for parents. Health visitors, community nurses, home liaison teachers, psychologists and (in some instances) volunteers have learned through using Portage how to work as a team; how to work directly with parents and share skills and expertise and, most importantly, to be able to offer parents positive action at a time when they feel depressed and pessimistic about happy outcomes.

Portage – are there problems in partnership?

Mittler and McConachie (1983) have documented the various parental preferences in terms of active participation in their children's development. As McConachie comments, 'Some parents are very enthusiastic about teaching their child in a structured way. Other parents want to pursue a more "natural" course of influencing their child and to leave teaching to the teachers. Others may find consistent special effort difficult to sustain'.

Critics of Portage have tended to focus on its potential to over-burden already stressed parents; to encourage parents to function in a strictly behavioural way and to ritualize parent/child interaction. However, such criticism neglects the central Portage resource of shared parent/professional goal setting; the sharing of professional skills *with* and not *on* parents and the opportunity for parent and home teacher to use their shared knowledge in other professional contexts. Many parents giving evidence to the Fish Committee stressed the apparent isolation and fragmentation of services for handicapped under-fives. All emphasized the value of home teaching programmes and most wished them to extend and 'bridge' their children (and themselves) into full-time school. A recent study of families using the Honeylands Family Support Unit (Brimblecombe and Russell, 1986) found parental emphasis on services as 'offering something positive to help the child' as well as helping *parents* develop confidence to be key factors in satisfaction with services.

Portage is, of course, part of a network of services for families with young handicapped children. It is compatible with day or respite care, parent groups and workshops, attendance at LEA nursery schools or classes. Goal setting can be adapted to parent variables and to parents' priorities. Parents can apply their recording and teaching skills in other contexts (and in health or social services settings). Professionals have to accept that the 'Portage package' is more than a 'cookbook' of recipes, to be rigidly applied and seldom modified. Many of the current criticisms reflect over-zealous adherence to the seductive magic of the 'little blue box' (the teaching cards): lack of professional liaison (Portage being a team approach); a failure to appreciate wider circumstances in a family's life which may influence any form of participation and perhaps indicate the need for counselling and preparation prior to direct involvement in any programme. Families, if seen as systems, experience growth, development – and periods of inactivity or conflict. They will be influenced by existing social networks and the strengths (or demands) of the extended family; by life-cycle events like marriages and divorces; redundancy or illness. All such influences will in turn affect problem-solving skills; health and energy levels; satisfaction with parenting a particular child.

All can be encompassed in Portage if appropriate. Conflicts will arise only if feelings are not shared and professionals are over-prescriptive.

Portage in a multi-cultural society

Professional and parental anxiety about underachievement of many children from minority ethnic groups is frequently expressed and, as noted in the Swann Report (1985), reflects the difficulties of developing community-based whole-school or team-based policies, which can provide 'a framework of commonly accepted values, practices and procedures' for all families and their service providers. The ILEA's Fish Committee (1985) also observed the difficulties encountered by some parents from different ethnic groups in understanding the rationale for services for handicapped children and in developing an active role in helping their own children. Although difficulties may be encountered because of linguistic and other practical problems, the Fish Committee also clearly identified the perception of many minority ethnic group parents (particularly from the Afro-Caribbean communities) that special services were 'labelling'. The Committee found that 57 per cent of these parents (as compared with 22 per cent of other parents) were unhappy with the way in which they were told about their children's difficulties. 42 per cent (as compared to 13 per cent of all parents) felt that they received insufficient information and help. Clearly such perceptions reflect fundamental anxieties about professionals' attitudes and opportunities for partnership. They also indicate the dangers of parental involvement programmes being perceived as labelling, negative and segregationist unless positive steps can be taken to begin a dialogue with parents from different cultural or ethnic backgrounds right from the start.

Portage appears to offer an important tool for such work. It can be flexible to family needs; the programme of necessity involves a number of professionals who can use their involvement as a training exercise within their own agency. Because Portage teaches parental responsibility, it has potential for avoiding parental expectations of being 'deskilled' or 'not respected' by professionals. It can also establish patterns of partnership *before* a child enters school and avoid the frequently expressed anxiety about 'anticipated failure' for 'black' children.

Although there has been little research or evaluation as yet of Portage as a method for working with minority ethnic group families, one initiative in Central Birmingham, working with Asian families (Bardsley and Perkins, 1985) suggests that it can offer a model framework. The Birmingham Portage project was run jointly by the health authority and Barnados and involved 22 families, 11 of whom were Asian. The project identified the importance of understanding Asian family structures (not least because of the different emphasis placed upon large families; the mother's role in the family and the presence of siblings and other relatives who could participate in teaching tasks). All but one family could only work through interpreters and the project team had, therefore, to provide special training and support for the interpreters in order to discuss visits; teach role plays and check the use of words. The skills of both home adviser and interpreter grew to meet the complex task of working through a third person without losing the spontaneity and flexibility of the Portage approach. The activity charts assumed a special and additional importance as a means for all concerned to monitor what was happening. The project identified certain broad distinctions in the Asian families. Attitudes to play involved little traditional 'play equipment' or toys, but there was ready availability of attention from adults. Hence teaching objectives requiring equipment meant that such equipment had to be brought into the home. Most importantly attention had to be paid to the differences amongst many Asian families with regard to child-rearing practices and attitudes to handicap. Bardsley and Perkins comment that Asian families had a different model of family routines, which did not necessarily mirror the essentially Mid-West lifestyle routines implicit in the traditional home teaching programmes. These differences were not barriers, but needed to be recognized in using Portage and in identifying appropriate targets for families. The Asian families, as opposed to their English counterparts, had the additional resource of larger extended families who could also participate in Portage activities (but by implication also needed to understand its goals).

Implications of Portage for parental/professional partnership in school, day-care adult services

The usefulness of the Portage model for wider application clearly lies in its comparative simplicity to both larger groups of *professionals* such as teachers or nurses, as well as to parents. Professionals may experience many of the parental dilemmas in working with children with special needs, not least conflicting demands upon time and energy; lack of ongoing support in assessment, goal setting and programme implementation. Professionals may also become depressed or anxious if progress is minimal and they lack regular contact with a key supporter. Portage, with its weekly feedback on the efficacy of the current programme and the need (if any) for modification is flexible and can take account of changes in family or professional circumstances, such as illness, parental difficulties or other curricular work with a child. Most importantly Portage is designed for growth and greatly facilitates recording with a purpose and systematic analysis of a particular child's problems. It is also a system which is explicable and comprehensible to a variety of professionals and parents.

Examples of the use of Portage outside the traditional under-fives settings include a programme at Whitefield School, London (McBride and Gant, 1982) in which a Portage programme has been used to develop participation between teachers and parents of children with moderate learning difficulties and the Heltwate

School Mainstream Support Service (Rider and Keogh, 1982) in which an adapted Portage model creates a support service for local infant and junior schools in the new town of Peterborough, developing resources already in use within Heltwate School (a special school in the same town). In both the latter cases, Portage is used to develop skills in teachers *and* parents who may have no existing expertise in working with children with special educational needs.

The evaluation of the Heltwate School mainstream support scheme suggests some important lessons for the growing number of children with special educational needs currently integrated in ordinary schools. First, the Portage model does not involve a shift of responsibility of 'deskilling' from the teachers in mainstream education. It can avoid unnecessary referral of a child with learning difficulties (and inevitably some application of responsibility for that child) by offering mainstream teachers access to local and systematic help. *Parents* can be fully involved and can quickly develop a realistic and honest relationship with their child's teacher, as well as carrying out activities at home. The scheme additionally enables a large number of teachers in mainstream schools to be aware of strategies for helping children with special educational needs in the ordinary classroom and to seek help earlier than might have been the case. Since Portage is based upon the principle of *parent* participation, its adaptation in an educational setting can directly involve teachers with parents and avoid the polarization and anxiety which can result if parents and teachers are unclear about their roles.

Goal setting is not, however, only an educational objective. Toogood (1982) described at a recent Portage Conference how Portage offers a helpful model for goal setting in locally-based NHS hospital units. The Old Rectory (a residential unit run by the Winchester Health Authority and caring for severely mentally and multiply handicapped children up to 16) has used the Portage model, convening weekly staff meetings to review teaching targets set the previous week; identify and resolve any problems arising from these targets and setting new goals for the coming week. The significance of this weekly team meeting lies in the involvement of the *care* staff who, like parents on most Portage schemes, will carry out most of the teaching, planning the teaching goals and discussing the most appropriate strategies for implementing them. Portage also offers important possibilities in helping staff in day care settings (including day nurseries and child minders) or in residential care settings (including foster family placements) to participate in individual programmes and, most importantly, to record their own day-to-day experiences of a child in a coherent and comprehensible way. The team approach, which lies at the core of the Portage model, is in itself a *training* facility and encourages confidence and competence impossible to develop through occasional one-off professional contacts.

A neglected area in terms of parent support and parent involvement has been that of work with families of adolescent or young adult people with social or educational needs. Many families need help in encouraging independence skills and more adult-appropriate behaviour. The interest in parent rights and satisfaction with services is being mirrored by a parallel concern about the rights and needs of young people and their right to 'speak for themselves'. Skill-sharing in the context of adolescence (with the attendant problems of the transition to adult life and services) also lends itself to the development of the Portage model, although innovative schemes for this age group are still thin on the ground. One example of an adapted use of the Portage model for adults is the Bereweeke skill-teaching system (Jenkins, 1982), which provides a way of organizing systematic individual teaching programmes for mentally handicapped people living in residential care. The system was developed and tested by the Wessex Health Care Evaluation Research Team, at Bereweeke House in Winchester (Jenkins *op. cit.*). Although designed for residential staff (and not for parents), the scheme has enormous significance not only as a means of giving young adults skills (with an assessment of current skills and deficits leading to the selection of a goal which will be useful to both the young person and those working with him or her) but of adapting a scheme primarily directed at *young* children to situations where the *resident* or client – as an adult – also has to consent to participate in the programme. The extension of Portage for *professionals* underlines the importance of not perceiving Portage as an under-fives induction course for other services. The Wessex experience clearly identifies the desire of parents to share the same quality of partnership when their children move on to school. Portage develops expectations which – if unmet – may lead to disappointment and alienation. 'Portage' parents will have developed confidence; the ability to observe their child objectively and a desire to be involved. Teachers, without support, may conversely perceive such parents as demanding and over-ambitious. A survey of Portage parents' views on the services received (Land, 1985) found that half of the parents specifically wanted follow-on into full-time education (although not necessarily at the same level of intensity). Parents recognized the importance of the psychological support to them as parents; of having their child's difficulties recognized; of a monitoring service for parental support, advice, reassurance and for the maintenance of incentive. 'Developmental assessments' after leaving Portage were felt important, as families felt they needed to continue to monitor progress. The desire for ongoing *relevant* assessment and for *shared* experiences of a child's developmental progress as well as difficulties clearly needs to be maintained in an educational setting. It also represents a model for parental involvement in the formal assessment procedures of the Education Act 1981.

Portage: A Personal Epilogue

Robert J. Cameron

The speed of development of the Portage home teaching model has taken most people (myself included) by surprise and it now feels most strange indeed to recall five sparkling spring days in April 1976 when the first Portage workshop was held in the somewhat unpromising setting of what was then called a 'subnormality hospital' in deepest Hampshire.

As a practising educational psychologist, specializing in work with mentally handicapped children, my first reactions to the Portage approach were somewhat mixed. The *parent teaching aspect* caused me few worries (although in 1976 colleagues in my own and allied disciplines looked somewhat askance on this component). Fortunately, I had already made the discovery that even with a modicum of help, e.g. suggesting realistic and concrete teaching objectives, some parents were able to work out teaching methods for helping their handicapped child to reach these objectives. Similarly, I was excited by the *Portage checklist,* one of the most detailed assessment devices which I had ever seen, and the *activity chart* seemed like a simple but elegant procedure for arriving at a suitably individualized teaching method for a child who had special needs.

What worried me most was the *recording procedure* – I was convinced that parents could never be taught to keep detailed daily records of their teaching. Imagine my amazement therefore when our three home teachers brought completed activity charts to the first staff meeting and proudly demonstrated that parents had not only recorded the daily progress of their child, but were actually able to respond to this data by making positive improvement suggestions for the teaching of future activities of a similar sort!

I was also bothered by the *positive monitoring component* of the Portage model. Until that point in time, I had never questioned the 'professional autonomy' aspect of my work and baulked a bit at the idea of putting my service delivery up for public scrutiny. However, less than three months later I was extolling the virtues of positive monitoring – professional growth, collective responsibility for problems, pre-emptive problem solving, etc. – to anyone who could listen to my enthusiastic entreaties.

It now appears as though my early discoveries about the Portage approach were later shared by many other parents, support professionals in the caring services, and LEA and health authority administrators and policy makers. As a result, the last decade has seen a dramatic spread of Portage schemes all over the UK and a potted history of Portage would read something as follows:

1969   US. Portage chosen as one of the 21 (out of 203) research proposals funded by the Bureau for the Education of the Handicapped under the Handicapped Children's Early Education Act.

1972   US. Office of Special Education provided funds for replication and effectiveness evaluation of the Portage model.

1975   US. Joint Dissemination and Review Panel of the United States Office of Education unanimously validated the Portage project as a model for dissemination and replication throughout the country.

1976   UK. Wessex and Welsh Portage research projects set up.

1980   UK. First National Portage Conference organized.

1983   UK. National Portage Association formed.

1984   US. Portage materials translated into eight different languages.
UK. More than 100 Portage services located in National Portage Survey.

1985   UK. Department of Education and Science made £1.2
       million from the educational support grant available for
       setting up new Portage schemes in England.

There are two points to highlight in this short but dramatic historical
overview. In the first place, some of the *educationally untypical*
features of Portage – clear procedures, well-designed materials and
a monitoring/evaluation component – do appear to have aided
replication in different contexts. (Too many innovations in
education do not seem to generalize beyond a specific school or
centre and/or particular group practitioners.) Secondly, the rapid
development indicates that the Portage approach both identified
and filled a *service vacuum* for families who had a pre-school child
with special educational needs. (See Cameron, 1984c.)

However, despite the unchallenged popularity of Portage as a
service for families of handicapped pre-schoolers, such success in
itself would not have merited a publication of this sort. The real
strength of Portage lies in its dynamic model of service delivery
within which the monitoring of accumulated data encourages self-
evaluation and this in turn leads to planned improvement. In short,
Portage practitioners will continue to see the other side of problems
as opportunities!

Acknowledgements

My personal thanks must go to Sandra Conway, secretary for
Advanced Professional Training in Educational Psychology
(University of Southampton) who uncomplainingly typed and
corrected many of the drafts which preceded each completed
chapter. I am also grateful to Lynne McFarland and Diana Hilton-
Jones from NFER-Nelson who wholeheartedly supported the
efforts of everyone involved in this publication and to Roda
Morrison, desk editor at NFER-Nelson, who edited the typescript.

References

AINSCOW, M. and TWEDDLE, D. (1979). *Preventing Classroom Failure: An Objectives Approach*. Chichester: John Wiley and Sons.

BANDURA, A. (1975). 'The ethics and social purposes of behaviour modification', *Annual Review of Behaviour Therapy and Practice*, 3, 13–20.

BARDSLEY, J. and PERKINS, E. (1985). 'Portage with Asian families in Central Birmingham'. In: DALY, B., ADDINGTON, J., KERFOOT, S. and SIGSTON, A. (Eds) *Portage: The Importance of Parents*. Windsor: NFER-NELSON.

BARNA, S., BIDDER, R., GRAY, O.P., CLEMENTS, J. and GARDNER, S. (1980). 'The progress of developmentally delayed pre-school children in a home training scheme', *Child: Care, Health and Development*, 6, 157–64.

BARNETT, B. (1985). 'The concept of "informed consent" and its use in the practice of psychology', *Education and Child Psychology*, 2, 2, 34–9.

BECKER, W.C., ENGELMANN, S., CARNINE, D.W. and RHINE, W.R. (1981). 'Direct Instruction Model'. In: RHINE, W.R. (Ed) *Making School More Effective: New Directions from Follow-Through*. New York: Academic Press.

BENDALL, S. (1985). 'National Portage Survey: preliminary results'. In: DALY, B., ADDINGTON, J., KERFOOT, S. and SIGSTON, A. (Eds) *Portage: The Importance of Parents*. Windsor: NFER-NELSON.

BENDALL, S., SMITH, J. and KUSHLICK, A. (1984). *National Study of Portage-type Home Teaching Services*. Vol. 1: Report; Vol. 2: Methodology and results; Vol. 3: Detailed reports of nineteen services visited. University of Southampton: Wessex Health Care Evaluation Research Team.

BIDDER, R., BRYANT, G. and GRAY, O.P. (1975). 'Benefits to Down's syndrome children through training their mothers'. *Archives of the Diseases of Children*, 50, 383–6.

BIDDER, R.T., HEWITT, K.E. and GRAY, O.P. (1982). 'Evaluation of teaching methods in a home-based training scheme for developmentally delayed preschool children', *Child: Care, Health and Development*, 9, 1–12.

BIJOU, S.W. (1955). 'A systematic approach to an experimental analysis of young children', *Child Development*, 26, 161–8.

BIJOU, S.W. (1957). 'Methodology for an experimental analysis of child behavior', *Psychological Reports*, 3, 243–50.

BIJOU, S.W. (1961). 'Rapid development of multiple schedule performances with children', *J. Experimental Analysis of Behavior*, 4, 7–16.

BLUMA, S., SHEARER, M., FROHMAN, A. and HILLIARD, J. (1976). *Portage Guide to Early Education: Checklist*. Windsor: NFER-NELSON.

BLUMENFELD, A. (1974). 'Ethical problems in child guidance', *British Journal of Medical Psychology*, 47, 17–26.

BOOTH, S. and JEWELL, T. (1983). 'Programmes for slow learners', *Journal of the Association of Educational Psychologists*, 6, 2, 58–61.

BOYD, R. (1977). *Final Report – Acquisition and Generalisation of Teaching and Child Management Behaviour in Parents of Handicapped Children. A Comparative Study*. Portage, Wisconsin: Portage Project, CESA 12.

BRICKER, D., BAILEY, E. and BRUDER, M.B. (1984). 'The efficiency of early intervention and the handicapped infant: a wise or wasted resource?' In: WOLRAICH, M. and ROUTH, D.K. (Eds) *Advances in Developmental and Behavioural Paediatrics*, 5, 373–423.

BRIMBLECOMBE, F.S.W. (1983). *Honeylands Progress Report*. Exeter Paediatric Research Unit, Royal Devon and Exeter Hospital.

BRIMBLECOMBE, F.S.W. and RUSSELL, P. (1986). *Honeylands – A Philosophy of Family Support*. In preparation.

BRONFENBRENNER, U. (1974). *Is Early Intervention Effective?* A report on longitudinal evaluations of preschool programmes. Vol. II. (DHEW Publication No. OHO 75–25). Washington, DC: US Dept. of Health, Education and Welfare.

BROSNAN, D. and HUGGETT, S. (1984). 'From checklists to curriculum – using Portage as a basis for curriculum development in nursery school'. In: DESSENT, T. (Ed) *What is Important about Portage?* Windsor: NFER-NELSON.

BUCKLEY, S. (1984). 'The influence of family variables on children's progress on Portage'. In: DESSENT, T. (Ed) *What is Important about Portage?* Windsor: NFER-NELSON.

BUCKLEY, S. (1985). 'Teaching parents to teach reading to teach language – a project with Down's children and their families'. In: TOPPING, K. and WOLFENDALE, S. (Eds) *Parental Involvement in Children's Reading*. London: Croom Helm.

BUTTERWORTH, G. (1984). Cognitive Problems in Infancy. Paper presented to the 'Association pour la recherche sur l'autisme et la psychose infantile'. Paris, France (November).

CALLIAS, M.M. and JENKINS, J. (1973). *Group Training in Behaviour Modification: A Pilot Project with Parents of Severely Retarded Children*. Unpublished.

CAMERON, J. (1984). 'A parent's view'. In: DESSENT, T. (Ed) *What is Important about Portage?* Windsor: NFER-NELSON.

CAMERON, R.J. (1979). 'A lot can happen at home too', *Journal of Remedial Education*, 14, 4, 173–8.

CAMERON, R.J. (1981). 'Curriculum development: clarifying and planning curriculum objectives', *Remedial Education*, 16, 4, 163–70.

CAMERON, R.J. (Ed) (1982). *Working Together: Portage in the UK.* Windsor: NFER-NELSON.

CAMERON, R.J. (1984a). 'Sharing expertise', *Where* (Journal of the Advisory Centre for Education), 194, 24–7.

CAMERON, R.J. (1984b). 'Extending Portage teaching: helping children to generalize and adapt skills'. In: DESSENT, T. (Ed) *What is Important about Portage?* Windsor: NFER-NELSON.

CAMERON, R.J. (1984c). 'Portage in the UK: 1984', *Journal of Community Education*, 3, 3, 24–33.

CAMERON, R.J. (1985a). 'A problem-centred approach to family problems'. In: DALY, B., ADDINGTON, J., KERFOOT, S. and SIGSTON, A. (Eds) *Portage: The Importance of Parents.* Windsor: NFER-NELSON.

CAMERON, R.J. (1985b). 'Parents as educators: learning from Portage'. In: PUGH, G. (Ed) *Working Together with Special Educational Needs: Implications for Preschool Services,* Partnership Papers III. London: National Children's Bureau.

CAMERON, R.J., CHAMBERS, G. and MARTIN, S. (1984). 'What is wrong with Portage?' *Health Visitor,* 57, 142–4.

CAMERON, R.J. and TEE, G. (1985). 'Teaching method: a model for pupils with and without special educational needs', *Educational and Child Psychology,* 2, 3, 145–9.

CARDOSO-MARTINS, C. and MERVIS, C.B. (1985). 'Maternal speech to prelinguistic children with Down's syndrome', *American Journal of Mental Deficiency,* 89, 5, 451–8.

CARNINE, D. (1979). 'Direct Instruction: a successful system for educationally high risk children', *Journal of Curriculum Studies,* 2, 1, 29–45.

CASTILLO, H., GLOSSOP, C., HALL, J., KUSHLICK, A. and SMITH, J. (1980). *The Wessex Portage Teaching Service: A Comparison of Service Standards 1976–79.* Research Report 154. University of Southampton: Wessex Health Care Evaluation Research Team.

CASTILLO, M., SMITH, J., GLOSSOP, C. and KUSHLICK, A. (1982). The Wessex Portage Project: Maintenance after Three Years. Research Report No. 154. University of Southampton: Wessex Health, Care and Evaluation Research Team.

CAVE, C. and MADDISON, P. (1978). *A Survey of Recent Research in Special Education.* Windsor: NFER-NELSON.

CLARK, I. and CAMERON, R.J. (1983). 'Helping handicapped children in a playgroup setting', *Contact* (Journal of the Preschool Playgroups Association), April, 17–19.

CLEMENTS, J., BIDDER, R., GARDNER, S., BRYANT, G. and GRAY, O.P. (1980). 'A home advisory service for pre-school children with developmental delays', *Child: Care, Health and Development,* 6, 25–33.

CLEMENTS, J., EVANS, C., JONES, C., OSBORNE, K. and UPTON, G. (1981). *The Development and Evaluation of an Assessment-linked Training Scheme for the Mentally Handicapped Child.* St Cadoc's Hospital, Gwent: Psychology Department.

COCHRANE, D.C. and SHEARER, D.E. (1984). 'The Portage model for home teaching'. In: PAINE, S.C., BELLAMY, G.T. and WILCOX, B. *Human Services that Work*. Baltimore, MD: Paul H. Brookes Publishing Co.

COOK, E. (1982). 'A Portage parent support scheme'. In: CAMERON, R.J. (Ed) *Working Together: Portage in the UK*. Windsor: NFER-NELSON.

COOPER, L. and HENDERSON, R. (Eds) (1973). *Something Wrong?* By parents of mentally handicapped children. London: Arrow Books.

COPLEY, M., BISHOP, M. and PORTER, J. (1986). *Portage: More Than a Teaching Programme?* Windsor: NFER-NELSON.

COURT, S.D.M. (Chairperson) (1976). *Fit for the Future*. Report of the Committee of Child Health Services. Cmnd 6684. London: HMSO.

COURTNEY, P. (1985). 'Using Portage with the severely mentally and visually handicapped'. In: DALY, B., ADDINGTON, J., KERFOOT, S. and SIGSTON, A. (Eds) *Portage: The Importance of Parents*. Windsor: NFER-NELSON.

CUNNINGHAM, C. (1977). 'Down's syndrome: a positive approach to parent and professional collaboration', *Health Visitor*, 50, 2, 32–6.

CUNNINGHAM, C. (1982). 'Portage is not a panacea', *Health Visitor*, April, 55, 254.

CUNNINGHAM, C. and DAVIS, H. (1985a). 'Early parent counselling'. In: CRAFT, M., BICKNESS, J. and HOLLINS, S. (Eds) *Mental Handicap, a Multidisciplinary Approach*. New York: Balliere Tindall.

CUNNINGHAM, C. and DAVIS, H. (1985b). *Working with Parents: Frameworks for Collaboration*. Milton Keynes: Open University Press.

CUNNINGHAM, C. and JEFFREE, D.M. (1971). *Working with Parents: Developing a Workshop Course for Parents of Young Mentally Handicapped Children*. Manchester: NSMHC/Hester Adrian Research Centre.

CUSWORTH, S.A. (1980). Kirklees Pre-Pilot Portage Evaluation Report. Huddersfield: Kirklees Education Department (mimeograph).

DALY, B. (1980). Evaluation of Portage Home Teaching. Pilot project, Report P/SOZ. Barking: Barking Education Department (mimeograph).

DALY, B. (1984). 'Report on the work of the National Portage Association Training and Monitoring Committee', *Portage Post*, 1, 6.

DALY, B. (1985). Editorial. In: DALY, B., ADDINGTON, J., KERFOOT, S. and SIGSTON, A., (Eds) *Portage: The Importance of Parents*. Windsor: NFER-NELSON.

DALY, B., ADDINGTON, J., KERFOOT, S. and SIGSTON, A. (Eds) (1985). *Portage: The Importance of Parents*. Windsor: NFER-NELSON.

DESSENT, T. (1984). *What is Important about Portage?* Windsor: NFER-NELSON.

DESSENT, T. (1985). 'Parentology: a critique', *Educational and Child Psychology*, 2, 1, 48–52.

DESSENT, S. and FERGUSON, L. (1984). 'First encounters with the multiply handicapped'. In: DESSENT, T. (Ed) *What is Important about Portage?* Windsor: NFER-NELSON.

DUNST, C.J., BRASSEL, W.R. and RHEINGROVER, R.M. (1982). 'Structural and organisational features of sensori-motor intelligence among retarded infants and toddlers', *British Journal of Educational Psychology*, 51, 133–43.

DYER, M. and HUGGETT, S. (1984). 'The Cedar School Project – one year on'. In: DESSENT, T. (Ed) *What is Important about Portage?* Windsor: NFER-NELSON.

EISENBERG, L. (1975). 'The ethics of intervention: acting amidst ambiguity', *J. Child Psychol. Psychiat.*, 16, 93–104.

ELLENDER, P. (1982). What can be learned from volunteers? A formative evaluation of a volunteer Portage group. MSc (Educational Psychology) dissertation, University of Southampton.

FAUPEL, A.W. (1986). 'Curriculum Management 2: Teaching curriculum objectives', *Educational Psychology in Practice*, 2,2. (In press.)

FAUPEL, A.W. and CAMERON, R.J. (1984). 'Self-directed teaching: the ultimate objective of direct instruction'. In: DESSENT, T. (Ed) *What is Important about Portage?* Windsor: NFER-NELSON.

FELCE, D., DE KOCK, U., MANSELL, J. and JENKINS, J. (1984). 'Providing systematic individual teaching for severely disturbed and profoundly handicapped mentally handicapped children in residential care', *Behaviour Research and Therapy*, 22, 3, 299–309.

FERGUSON, N. and WATT, J. (1980). 'Professionals and the parents of mentally handicapped children', *Bulletin of the British Psychological Society*, 33, 59–60.

FERSTER, C.B. and DE MEYER, M.K. (1961). 'The development of performances in autistic children in an automatically controlled environment', *Journal of Chronic Diseases*, 13, 312–45.

FISH, J. (Chairperson) (1985). *Educational Opportunities for All?* Report of the Committee reviewing provision to meet special educational needs. London: Inner London Education Authority.

FOX, A.M. (1973). *'They Get This Training But They Don't Really Know How You Feel'*. Transcripts of interviews with parents of handicapped children. London: Action Research for the Crippled Child.

FOXEN, T. and MCBRIEN, J. (1981). *The EDY Inservice Course for Mental Handicap Practitioners: Training Staff in Behavioural Methods.* (a) Instruction Handbook, (b) Trainee Workbook. Manchester: University Press.

FREDERICKSON, N. and HARAN, H. (1986). 'Portage evaluation and re-evaluation: a day nursery project', *Educational Psychology in Practice*, 1, 4, 159–65.

GARDNER, J. and JUDSON, S. (1982). 'Planning long-term curriculum objectives and getting the sequence right'. In: CAMERON, R.J. (Ed) *Working Together: Portage in the UK.* Windsor: NFER-NELSON.

GARDNER, J.M. (1980). *Developmentally Sequenced Checklists of Portage Guide to Early Education.* Walsall: School Psychological Service.

GARDNER, W.I. (1977). *Learning and Behaviour Characteristics of*

Exceptional Children and Youth: A Humanistic Behavioural Approach.
London: Allyn and Bacon.
GATH, A. (1978). *Down's Syndrome and the Family: The Early Years.*
London: Academic Press.
GLENDENNING, C. (1983). *Unshared Care – Parents and their Disabled
Children.* London: Routledge and Kegan Paul.
GLOSSOP, C. and CASTILLO, O. (1982). 'Extending the Portage model
(research)'. In: CAMERON, R.J. (Ed) *Working Together: Portage in the
UK.* Windsor: NFER-NELSON.
GRAY, S.W. and WANDERSON, L.P. (1980). 'The methodology of home-based
intervention studies: problems and promising strategies', *Child
Development,* 51, 993–1009.
GRIFFITHS, M. and RUSSELL, P. (Eds) (1985). *Working Together with
Handicapped Children: Guidelines for Parents and Professionals.*
London: Souvenir Press.

HALLMARK, N. (1983). 'A support service to primary schools'. In: BOOTH, T.
and POTTS, P. (Eds) *Integrating Special Education.* Oxford: Blackwell.
HALLMARK, N. and DESSENT, A. (1982). 'A special education service centre',
Special Education: Forward Trends, 9, 1, 6–8.
HARING, N., LOVITT, T., EATON, M. and HANSON, C. (1978). *The Fourth R –
Research in the Classroom.* Columbus, Ohio: Charles E. Merrill.
HEDDERLEY, R. and JENNINGS, K. (1986). *Extending and Developing
Portage.* Windsor: NFER-NELSON. (In press.)
HEWETT, S. (1970). *The Family and the Handicapped Child.* London: Allen
and Unwin.
HEWSON, S., MCCONKEY, R. and JEFFREE, D. (1980). 'The relationship
between structured and free play in the development of a mentally
handicapped child: a case study', *Child: Care, Health and Development,*
6, 2, 73–82.
HMSO (1980). Behaviour Modification. Report of a Joint Working Party to
Formulate Ethical Guidelines for the Conduct of Programmes of
Behaviour Modification in the National Health Service. London:
HMSO.
HOLLAND, F.L.U. and NOAKS, J.C. (1982). 'Portage in Mid-Glamorgan:
description and comment on this pre-school home intervention scheme',
Journal of Association of Educational Psychologists, 5, 9, 32–7.
HONIG, A.S. (1980). 'Parent involvement and the development of children
with special needs', *Early Child Development and Care,* 6, 179–99.
HOWLIN, P., MARCHANT, R., RUTTER, M., BERGER, M., HERSOV, L. and YULE,
W. (1973). 'A home-based approach to the treatment of autistic
children', *Journal of Autism and Childhood Schizophrenia,* 3, 308–36.
HUGGETT, S. and DYER, M. (1982). 'Checklists, curriculum planning and
assessment: using Portage to develop a curriculum in a special school
nursery class'. In: CAMERON, R.J. (Ed) *Working Together: Portage in the
UK.* Windsor: NFER-NELSON.

JENKINS, J. (1982). 'The Bereweeke skill teaching system'. In: CAMERON, R.J. (Ed) *Working Together: Portage in the UK*. Windsor: NFER-NELSON.

JENKINS, J., MANSELL, J. and FELCE, D. (1983). *The Bereweeke Skill-Teaching System: Assessment Checklist*. Windsor: NFER-NELSON.

JESIEN, G. (1983). Preschool intervention programmes in developing countries: why and one example of how. Unpublished MS. Portage, Wisconsin: Portage Project, CESA 12.

JESIEN, G. (1984). 'Home-based early intervention: a description of the Portage project model'. In: SCRATTON, D. (Ed) *Management of the Motor Disorders of Children with Cerebral Palsy*. Oxford: Blackwell Scientific Publications (in conjunction with Spastics International Medical Publications).

JESIEN, G., ALIAGE, J. and HAYNES, M. (1979). Validation of the Portage Model in Peru. Paper presented at the Inter-American Congress of Psychology. Lima (July).

JEWELL, T. and BOOTH, T. (1985). 'A 'Portage-style' system for supporting children with learning difficulties in normal schools'. In: DALY, B., ADDINGTON, J., KERFOOT, S., and SIGSTON, A. (Eds) *Portage: The Importance of Parents*. Windsor: NFER-NELSON.

JONES, M.E.O., BELL, A., PRYCE, G.J. and WOOD, P. (1979). 'Teaching the parents to help the child', *Nursing Mirror,* May 24, 26–8.

JONES, O.H.M. (1980). 'Prelinguistic communication skills in Down's syndrome and normal infants'. In: FIELD, T.M. (Ed) *High Risk Infants and Children: Adult and Peer Interactions*. New York: Academic Press.

KARASU, T. (1981). 'Ethical aspects of psychotherapy'. In: BLOCH, S. and CHODOFF, P. (Eds) *Psychiatric Ethics*. Oxford: Oxford University Press.

KUSHLICK, A. (1984). 'A National Portage Association?' In: DESSENT, T. (Ed) *What is Important about Portage?* Windsor: NFER-NELSON.

KUSHLICK, A., FELCE, D., and LUNT, B. (1978). Monitoring the effectiveness of services for severely handicapped people: implications for managerial and professional accountability. Paper presented at Annual Conference of the Association for Special Education (Liverpool, 1978). In: JACKSON, R. (Ed) *Wessex Studies in Special Education*. No. 13. Winchester: King Alfred's College.

KUSHLICK, A., SMITH, J. and GOLD, A. (1985). 'An intervention package to teach parents of severely retarded and severely non-compliant children and adults at home to teach their children new relevant skills'. In: DALY, B., ADDINGTON, J., KERFOOT, S. and SIGSTON, A. (Eds) *Portage: The Importance of Parents*. Windsor: NFER-NELSON.

LAING, A.F. (1979). *Young Children with Special Needs*. Swansea University: Department of Education.

LAND, A. (1985). 'Portage: parents' views', *Educational Psychology in Practice,* 1, 3, 120–3.

LANSDOWNE, R. (1980). *More than Sympathy: the Everyday Needs of Sick and Handicapped Children and their Families*. London: Tavistock Publications.

LE POIDEVIN, S. (1986). 'A model of disability rehabilitation counselling'. In: COPLEY, M., BISHOP, M. and PORTER, J. (Eds) *Portage: More Than a Teaching Programme?* Windsor: NFER-NELSON.

LE POIDEVIN, S. and CAMERON, J. (1985). 'Is there more to Portage than education?' In: DALY, B., ADDINGTON, J., KERFOOT, S. and SIGSTON, A. (Eds) *Portage: The Importance of Parents.* Windsor: NFER-NELSON.

LILLIE, D. (1981). 'Educational and psychological strategies for working with parents'. In: PAUL, J.L. (Ed) *Understanding and Working with Parents of Children with Special Needs.* New York: Holt, Rinehart and Winston.

LINDSAY, G. (1985). 'Integration: possibilities, practice and pitfalls', *Educational and Child Psychology,* 2, 3, 4–7.

LISTER, T. (1985). 'Portage – eight years on'. In: DALY, B., ADDINGTON, J., KERFOOT, S. and SIGSTON, A. (Eds) *Portage: The Importance of Parents.* Windsor: NFER-NELSON.

LISTER, T.A.J. and CAMERON, R.J. (1986). 'Curriculum Management (Part 1): Planning curriculum objectives', *Educational Psychology in Practice,* 2, 1, 6–14.

LLOYD, J. (1986). *Jacob's Ladder: a Parent's View of Portage.* Tunbridge Wells, Kent: Costello Educational.

LLOYD-BOSTOCK, S. (1976). 'Parents' experiences of official help and guidance in caring for a mentally handicapped child', *Child: Care, Health and Development,* 2, 325–38.

LORENZ, S. (1986). *Portage in Nurseries: a Workshop for Teachers and Nursery Nurses.* Salford: School Psychological Service.

LOVASS, O.I. (1985). *Behavioural Treatment and Recovery in Young Autistic Children.* Unpublished interim research report. Los Angeles: University of California.

MCBRIDE, L. and GANT, F. (1982). 'Short-term goal setting for mildly handicapped pupils'. In: CAMERON, R.J. (Ed) *Working Together: Portage in the UK.* Windsor: NFER-NELSON.

MCCONACHIE, H. (1983). 'Fathers, mothers, siblings: how do they see themselves?' In: MITTLER, P. and MCCONACHIE, H. (Eds) *Parents, Professionals and Mentally Handicapped People: Approaches to Partnership.* London: Croom Helm.

MCCONKEY, R. (1981). 'Education without understanding', *Special Education: Forward Trends,* 8, 3, 8–10.

MAY, G.J., MCALLISTER, J., RISLEY, T., TWARDOSZ, S., COX, C.H. *et al.* (1974). *Florida Guidelines for the Use of Behavioural Procedures in State Programs for the Retarded.* Florida State University Psychology Dept.

MAY, E. and SCHORTINGHUIS, N. (1984). 'Ten problems frequently encountered when using behavioural checklists'. In: ZEIGER, J.D. (Ed) *A Parent-focussed, Home Based, Headstart Handbook for Home Visitors.* Portage, Wisconsin: Headstart Training Centre – Portage Project, CESA 12.

MILLER, A., JEWELL, T., BOOTH, S. and ROBSON, D. (1985). 'Delivering educational programmes to slow learners', *Educational Psychology in Practice,* 1, 3, 99–104.

MITTLER, P. (1979). Parents as Partners in the Education of their Handicapped Children. Paper commissioned by UNESCO ED/79/ Conf. 606/7. Paris: UNESCO.

MITTLER, P. and MCCONACHIE, H. (1983). *Parents, Professionals and Mentally Handicapped People: Approaches to Partnership.* London: Croom Helm.

MITTLER, P. and MITTLER, H. (1982). *Partnership with Parents.* London: UNESCO.

MYATT, R. (1983). *Report of the Independent Evaluation of the South Lakeland Preschool Advisory Service.* Kendal, Cumbria: Westmorland Society for the Mentally Handicapped.

NATIONAL PORTAGE ASSOCIATION (1985). *A Guide for Setting up a Portage Service.* Obtainable from NPA Information and Publicity Committee, Room 235, Department of Psychology, The University, Southampton SO9 5NH.

OAKLEY, A. (1974). *The Sociology of Housework.* Oxford: Martin Robertson.

OLENICK, D.L. and PEAR, J.P. (1980). 'Differential reinforcement of correct responses to probes and prompts in picture name training with severely retarded children', *Journal of Applied Behaviour Analysis,* 13, 77–89.

PAHL, J. and QUINE, E. (1984). *Families with Mentally Handicapped Children: A Study of Stress and a Service Response.* University of Kent: Canterbury Health Services Research Unit.

PALMER, C. and HUGGETT, S. (1985). 'Electrifying Portage'. In: DALY, B., ADDINGTON, J., KERFOOT, S. and SIGSTON, A. (Eds) *Portage: The Importance of Parents.* Windsor: NFER-NELSON.

PENISTON, E. (1972). An evaluation of the Portage project. Unpublished MS. Portage, Wisconsin: Portage Project, CESA 12.

PHILPS, C. (1984). *Elizabeth Joy, 'a Mother's Story': the Pain and Joy of a Down's Baby.* Tring, Herts.: Lion Publishing.

PILLING, D. (1973). *The Handicapped Child: Studies in Child Development Research Review.* Vol. III. London: Longman in association with the National Children's Bureau.

PILLING, D. (1981). 'The family with a handicapped child: a review of research', *Highlight.* No. 42. London: National Children's Bureau.

PLOWDEN, B. (Chairperson) (1967). *Children and their Primary Schools.* London: HMSO.

PORTAGE PROJECT (1975). *A Home Approach to the Early Education of Handicapped Children in Rural Areas.* Report presented to the US Office of Education Joint Dissemination Review Panel, Washington, DC.

POWELL, L. and PERKINS, E. (1984). 'Asian families with a pre-school handicapped child: a study', *Mental Handicap,* 12, June, 50–2.

PROSSER, M. (1982). 'No-one is screaming about these children', *Times Educational Supplement,* March 12th, 21.

REID, K. (1979). *Whose Children: the Interface of Medical, Social and Educational Facilities for ESN (S)*. Porthcawl, Glamorgan: Spastics Aid Society.

REMINGTON, B., LIGHT, P. and PORTER, D. (1981). 'A comparison of two methods of training symbol-object matching skills in non-speaking severely mentally retarded children', *Behaviour Research of Severe Developmental Disabilities*, 2, 157–74.

REVILL, S. and BLUNDEN, R. (1978). Home training of preschool children with developmental delay: a report of the development and evaluation of the replication of the Portage service in Ceredigion Health District, Dyfed. Research Report No. 5. Cardiff: Mental Handicap in Wales – Applied Research Unit.

REVILL, S. and BLUNDEN, R. (1979a). 'A home training service for preschool developmentally handicapped children', *Behaviour Research and Therapy*, 17, 3, 207–14.

REVILL, S. and BLUNDEN, R. (1979b). *Home Training of Preschool Children with Developmental Delay*. Report of the development and evaluation of the replication of the Portage Service in Ceredigion Health District, Dyfed. Report No. 5. University of Wales: Mental Handicap in Wales – Applied Research Unit.

RIDER, C. and KEOGH, P. (1982). 'The Heltwate School mainstream support service: an extension of Portage model'. In: CAMERON, R.J. (Ed) *Working Together: Portage in the UK*. Windsor: NFER-NELSON.

RISLEY, T. and WOLF, M. (1967). 'Establishing functional speech in echolalic children', *Behaviour Research and Therapy*, 5, 73–88.

ROBIN, M. and JOSSER, D. (1984). 'Maternal language and the development of successive infant identities', *Early Child Development and Care*, 17, 2/3, 167–77.

RUSSELL, P. (1983). 'The parents' perspective of family needs and how to meet them'. In: MITTLER, P. and MCCONACHIE, H. (Eds) *Parents, Professionals and Mentally Handicapped People: Approaches to Partnership*. London: Croom Helm.

RUSSELL, P. (1985). 'Portage – partnership with parents'. In: DALY, B., ADDINGTON, J., KERFOOT, S. and SIGSTON, A. (Eds) *Portage: The Importance of Parents*. Windsor: NFER-NELSON.

SAMPSON, N. (1984). Parents, preschoolers and Portage: an investigation of parents' views of Portage and a comparison of attitudes of parents with 'handicapped' and 'normal' children. Unpublished MSc (Child Development) dissertation. London: Institute of Education.

SANDOW, S. (1984). 'The Portage Project: ten years on'. In: DESSENT, T. (Ed) *What is Important about Portage?* Windsor: NFER-NELSON.

SANDOW, S. and CLARKE, A.D.B. (1978). 'Home intervention with parents of severely subnormal preschool children: an interim report', *Child: Care, Health and Development*, 4, 29–39.

SCHORTINGHUIS, E. and FROHMAN, A. (1974). 'A comparison of paraprofessional and professional success with preschool children', *Journal of Learning Disabilities*, 7, 245–7.

SHEARER, D.E. and LOFTIN, C.R. (1984). 'The Portage project: teaching parents to teach their preschool children in the home'. In: DANGEL, R.F. and POLSTON, R.A. (Eds) *Parent Training.* New York: The Guildford Press.

SHEARER, M.S. and SHEARER, D.E. (1972). 'The Portage Project: a model for early childhood education', *Exceptional Children,* 39, 3, 210–17.

SMITH, C. (1983). A social cognitive approach to developmental handicap: beyond Portage. Paper presented at London Conference of British Psychological Society (December).

SMITH, C. (1984). Intervention groups for handicapped infants and their parents. Unpublished discussion paper. Southampton Paediatric Department, Southampton General Hospital.

SMITH, J., KUSHLICK, A. and GLOSSOP, C. (1977). *The Wessex Portage Project: a Home Teaching Service for Families with a Pre-school Mentally Handicapped Child.* Research Report No. 125. Part I: Report; Part II: Appendices. University of Southampton: Wessex Health Care Evaluation Research Team.

SPAIN, B. and WIGLEY, G. (1975). *Right from the Start.* London: National Society for Mentally Handicapped Children.

STRATFORD, R.J. and COYNE, G. (1986). 'EDY meets Portage: the case for an arranged marriage', *Educational Psychology in Practice*, 2,2. (In press.)

STURMEY, P. (1986). 'The implications of research for the future development of Portage'. In: HEDDERLY, R. and JENNINGS, K. (Eds) *Extending and Developing Portage.* Windsor: NFER-NELSON. (In press.)

SWANN (Chairperson) (1985). *Education for All.* Report of the Committee of Inquiry into the education of children from minority ethnic groups. London: HMSO.

TAYLOR, T. (Chairperson) (1977). *A New Partnership in our School.* London: HMSO.

THARP, R.G. and WETZEL, R.J. (1969). *Behavior Modification in the Natural Environment.* New York and London: Academic Press.

THOMAS, G. (1985). 'What psychology had to offer education – then', *Bulletin of the British Psychological Society,* 38, 322–6.

TIZARD, J. and GRAD, J.C. (1961). *The Mentally Handicapped and Their Families: A Social Survey.* London: Oxford University Press.

TJOSSEM, T.D. (1976). 'Early intervention: issues and approaches'. In: TJOSSEM, T.D. (Ed) *Intervention Strategies for High Risk Infants and Young Children.* Baltimore: University Park Press.

TOOGOOD, A. (1982). 'Goal setting in a locally-based hospital unit'. In: CAMERON, R.J. (Ed) *Working Together: Portage in the UK.* Windsor: NFER-NELSON.

TOPPING, K. and WOLFENDALE, S. (1985). *Parental Involvement in Children's Reading.* London: Croom Helm.

TYERMAN, C. and SEWPAUL, C. (1983). 'Portage: its extension and use with adults', *Mental Handicap,* 11, September, 120–1.

VICARY, S. (1985). 'Observations of mothers interacting with their developmentally delayed one-year-olds'. In: DALY, B., ADDINGTON, J., KERFOOT, S. and SIGSTON, A. (Eds) *Portage: The Importance of Parents.* Windsor: NFER-NELSON.

WAHLER, R.G., WINKEL, G.H., PETERSON, R.F. and MORRISON, D.C. (1965). 'Mothers as behaviour therapists for their own children', *Behaviour Research and Therapy,* 3, 113–24.

WARNOCK, M. (Chairperson) (1978). *Special Educational Needs.* Report of the Committee of Inquiry into the education of handicapped children and young people, Cmnd 7212. London: HMSO.

WATSON, L.S. and BASSINGER, J.F. (1974). 'Parent training technology: a potential delivery system', *Mental Retardation,* 12, 3–10.

WHITE, K. (1979). 'One area where home visits are to be encouraged', *Medical News,* December 13th, 14–15.

WHITE, M. (1984a). Using remedial teaching based on the Portage Model at Weeke Infant School. Unpublished Report to Winchester Portage Management Team. Available from Winchester Portage Home Teaching Service, Silverhill, Winchester, SO23 8AF, Hampshire.

WHITE, M. (1984b). 'A new look at language teaching through the Portage project'. In: DESSENT, T. (Ed) *What is Important about Portage?* Windsor: NFER-NELSON.

WHITE, M. (1985). Setting up conditions for play. Main speaker presentation at National Portage Association, Eastern Region, Study Day. Institute of Education, Cambridge (June).

WHITE, M. (1986). 'Educating the young child: support for the parent as teacher'. In: COPLEY, M., BISHOP, M. and PORTER, J. (Eds) *Portage: More Than a Teaching Programme?* Windsor: NFER-NELSON.

WHITE, M. and EAST, K. (1983). *The Wessex Revised Portage Language Checklist.* Windsor: NFER-NELSON.

WHITE, M. and EAST, K. (1986). 'Selecting early objectives in language', *Educational Psychology in Practice* 2, 1, 15–22.

WHITTAKER, S. (1985). 'Can all parents teach their own children?' *Mental Handicap,* 13, 49–50.

WIEHL, P. (1986). 'Portage in Bradford: training volunteers'. In: HEDDERLY, R. and JENNINGS, K. *Extending and Developing Portage.* Windsor: NFER-NELSON. (In press).

WILKIN, D. (1979). *Caring for the Mentally Handicapped Child.* London: Croom Helm.

WOLF, M., RISLEY, T. and MEES, H. (1964). 'Application of operant conditioning to the behaviour problems of an autistic child', *Behaviour Research and Therapy,* 1, 305–12.

WOLFENDALE, S. (1983). *Parental Participation in Children's Development and Education.* London: Gordon and Breach Science Publishers.

WOLFENDALE, S. (1984). 'Description of parental profiling and the parental contribution'. In: *Assessment.* Down's Children's Association, 1, 2, Summer.

WOLFENDALE, S. (1985a). 'A review of parental involvement and the place of Portage'. In: DALY, B., ADDINGTON, J., KERFOOT, S. and SIGSTON, A.

(Eds) *Portage: The Importance of Parents.* Windsor: NFER-NELSON.

WOLFENDALE, S. (1985b). 'Parental Profiling and the Parental Contribution to Section 5 (Education Act, 1981) Assessment and Statementing Procedures', Newsletter of the Association of Child Psychology and Psychiatry, 7, 2, April.

WOLFENDALE, S. (1985c). 'Parental Contribution to Section 5 (Education Act 1981) Assessment Procedures'. Report by the working group on the national pilot exercise and feasibility study 1984–85. Psychology Department, North East London Polytechnic.

WOLFENDALE, S. (1985d). 'Parental involvement in children's development and education: an overview', *Educational and Child Psychology*, 2, 1, 3–9.

WOLKIND, S. (1981). 'Depression in mothers of young children', *Archives of Diseases in Childhood,* 56, 1–3.